RAISING COMPETENT
TEENAGERS

RAISING COMPETENT
TEENAGERS

...IN AN AGE OF PORN, DRUGS AND TATTOOS

DR. LINDA FRIEDLAND

ROCKPOOL
PUBLISHING

A Rockpool book
PO Box 252
Summer Hill
NSW 2130
Australia
www.rockpoolpublishing.com.au
http://www.facebook.com/RockpoolPublishing

First published in 2013 by Tafelberg
an imprint of NB Publishers, a division of Media24 Boeke (Pty) Ltd
40 Heerengracht, Cape Town 8001

National Library of Australia Cataloguing-in-Publication entry

Friedland, Linda, author.
Raising Competent Teenagers: ...in an age of porn, drugs and tattoos / Dr
Linda Friedland.
9781925017397 (paperback)

Includes index.

Parenting.
Parent and teenager.
Teenagers — Family relationships.
Teenagers — Drug use — Prevention.
Adolescent psychology.

649.125

Cover design by Jessica Le
Editor: Mark Ronan
Proofreader: Vanessa Vineall
Indexer: Anna Tanneberger
Typography: Jean van der Meulen
Printed in China by Everbest Printing
10 9 8 7 6 5 4 3 2

CONTENTS

FOREWORD

PARENTING IS LIKE GOLF. Just as there are three distinct parts to a golf hole, there are three different parenting stages.

Each requires something different from you.

You start by hitting the ball off the tee, usually with a wood, which is relatively straightforward. Your total focus is on hitting the ball off the tee cleanly to give yourself the best possible approach to the hole. This is akin to early childhood, when the parents' focus is on getting their children off to a good start in life. There's pressure at this stage, but it's manageable.

In golf, the walk down the fairway after your initial tee shot is generally enjoyable. You can replace the wood with a number of irons, which are easier to use. There's plenty of margin for error as a fluffed shot on the fairway doesn't matter too much. This part of the hole is like parenting children from four years of age through to ten. It's a more relaxed period for parents: children are generally fairly malleable, and the rewards are high in terms of the pride you can take in your children's achievements, the enjoyable time you spend as a family and the affection you receive from children in this age group.

After the relative ease of the fairway, the green looms on the horizon and suddenly you need to up your game. There are water hazards and sand traps everywhere. You replace your trusty irons with your putter and now every shot counts. The pressure ramps up and before you know it, you are playing a very different game. It's challenging and you need to concentrate on every shot.

Similarly, most parents of teenagers find they must adapt to greater pressures. As they demand more freedom, teenagers are less pliable and more likely to challenge you and your authority. You need to use different communication tools if you are going to get through to them and help them navigate the risks and hazards they face. Just as a golfer must change his or her game around the green, you need to adapt if you are going to stay in the parenting game with your young person.

Dr Linda Friedland has produced a fabulous manual to help mums and dads adapt to the modern parenting game. It's eminently practical, wise, time-saving and very down to earth. I applaud Linda for distilling the wisdom of many prominent parenting educators, and faithfully drawing on their thoughts and advice throughout this great book. Her own voice can be clearly heard too, both as a medical practitioner and a parent.

You will find that the information she presents is very current, and organised into bite-sized, easy-to-read chunks. Just like the book's title, many of the topics she covers, such as pornography, cyber bullying and tattoos, may make you feel a little uncomfortable but they are topics that need addressing if you want to stay in the game with today's young people.

There are two ways to approach *Raising Competent Teenagers..in an age of porn, drugs and tattoos.* You can use it as a 'how-to' guide, reading it from start to finish so you feel empowered and informed as a parent. Alternatively, you can approach it as a problem-solver, dipping into its wisdom when you find yourself scratching your head, wondering what to do next with the young person in your family. Either way, this book deserves a prominent spot beside the bed of any person who has a teenager in their life!

Importantly, Linda Friedland places authority in the hands of you, the parent, and encourages you to be a confident, compassionate leader as you raise your young person through the potentially tricky years of adolescence. Enjoy the journey.

Michael Grose
Director, Parentingideas.com.au
November 2012

AUTHOR'S NOTE

PARENTING IS SIMPLY DEFINED AS the 'act of raising a child' and yet nothing can adequately prepare us for this major task. I am still in the midst of it: my two youngest children are teenagers; the older three are in their early 20s. Although much of the distress of adolescence attracts a great deal of attention and even media awareness, I don't believe raising teenagers has to be an entirely awful experience. I think much of it can in fact be trouble free and at times even quite satisfying. There is a wonderful African proverb – it takes a village to raise a child. There are many things and people other than you, the parents, that influence your child's development. Struggling with challenging adolescents is no less daunting than dealing with toddlers. Remember that adolescence is a life stage and most testy teens grow into wonderful adults, but they do require healthy parenting, strong role models, love and patience to get through this stage. We often judge ourselves harshly when it comes to parenting, but there are many types of parents and various ways to parent well. Let go of the guilt and self-blame. It is never too late. This book will hopefully give you some new insights and perspectives on parenting teenagers, supported by views and data from some of the world's leading parenting experts.

Note: Throughout the book, I have chosen to interchange gender and make use of both 'he' and 'she' when describing teenagers.

INTRODUCTION: BODY PIERCINGS AND OTHER POWER STRUGGLES

IT WAS AN UNUSUALLY HOT day as we trampled through the African bush, trying to avoid thorns scratching against bare legs, and treading carefully over potential snake pits. We hadn't anticipated the walk would take so long and were looking forward to the end of the incessant 'are we there yets?', grumbled by the youngest boys. My then 13-year-old daughter decided it was a good time to engage in an important conversation. She obviously believed that in the middle of this arduous hike, I would be worn down enough to simply say 'yes, sure'. She wasn't entirely wrong. 'Mum, can I get a belly ring?'

'Oh, yeah, sure!' was my sarcastic response, 'as long as Dad says it's okay,' knowing full well what his response would be: 'Not a chance!'

So off she trotted a hundred metres ahead to where Dad was leading the hike into a herd of zebras. Two minutes later, she ran jubilantly back to me as I continued dragging myself up the hill with two small, exhausted hikers in tow. 'Dad says it's fine!'

'What!? Well it's absolutely NOT fine. Dad's wrong or joking, and I say no. No way. There is no way that you are getting a belly ring. The final answer is no.'

The whys and wherefores continued for a short while. But then silence ensued. There is no doubt that my thinking was wavering somewhat, but not my resolve. It was crystal clear to me in that moment that (in my book of rules) a belly ring was entirely inappropriate for a 13-year-old. But I also knew that, although I am not fond of body piercings at all, in choosing my battles, body piercing (a few select types only) is not one of the absolute non-negotiables.

'How is this plan, Leigh?' I continued. 'When you are 16, we will revisit this conversation, and if you are still keen on the belly ring, I will take you to get it done.'

At the time, she obviously wasn't happy with my response, didn't believe the 16-year-old part of the plan and was infuriated by my initial sarcasm. She gave me the most unpleasant 'I hate you' glare. By the way, she has an extremely fierce stare, which she has inherited from her dad, and which has more to do with the shape of their eyebrows and foreheads than genuine disdain. But on this particular occasion, she was certainly using those facial features to her advantage and intended to show me how angry she felt. It is the kind of look an adolescent girl will use on a friend after being extremely hurt. It is the kind of look that says 'it's over, you are not my friend'. I received her message loud and clear. In that moment I also realised that this was an important crossroads in our relationship. I would have to choose to do the right thing over being popular. I glared back at her and shared with her the difficult words that needed to be said: 'I know you are angry with me. I know right now you don't like me at all. But I am not your friend. I am your mother. I am here to love you, but I am also here to guide you in what I feel is correct. If by standing my ground and doing what is right, you continue to dislike me, I will live with it. If I can never be your friend, it may be painful for me. But my role is as your mother. You may hate me for some things, but I cannot give up on what I think is best for you in order to be your friend.'

When I decided to begin writing this book, it was on her and her twin sister Elle's 21st birthday that I reminded Leigh of this incident. As we chuckled about it, she blurted out: 'But you've left out the most important part of the story! The real significance of this story is what you did three years later,' she asserted. 'You need to share with your readers how you took both me and Elle to the piercing parlour to get the belly-ring piercing, as promised. You need to include how all our friends went behind their mums' backs, had the belly piercing and then hid it from their parents. You kept your word about my 16th birthday.

You investigated the different piercing parlours until you found the most clinical and sterile environment that met with your medical standards, inspected the instruments, ensured they used disposable needles and gloves, and then went on to almost perform the procedure yourself.'

And what Leigh forgets is that as we waited, she became quite squeamish witnessing the piercing procedure on someone else. She even asked if we could please leave and come back another day. We eventually went back, she had the piercing done, inserted a small belly ring and it really ceased to be a significant issue. Elle also decided to have a tiny nose ring inserted at the time.

Against the backdrop of my most challenging life experiences, raising teenagers has certainly not been the worst. Newborn infants, medical studies and internships, and moving country have ranked as far more stressful. I personally enjoy the teen years – the transition of a child into an adolescent, and guiding and witnessing the emergence of an adult. I think as parents today, we have become obsessed with early child-hood, as well as performance and outcomes. I also believe that we have possibly lost the way and the courage when it comes to taking charge in the teenage years. This book is not about adolescent psychol-ogy or theory. Although most of my books have been written wearing my medical hat, this book has me wearing the hat of my 25 years of parenting. I have written these pages with honesty and frankness but always backed up by sound research and the best expert opinions. Through a few personal anecdotes as well as those of patients and clients – and many fictitious examples too – the focus of this book is how best to handle each situation, and how best to raise a child into a quality adult in the midst of this totally new world order. Yes, our Y- and Z-generation teenagers may be internet based and high tech, but they desperately require our reality-based and high-touch parenting.

A NEW LIFE STAGE

ADOLESCENCE IS NOT JUST A period of dramatic physical growth and pubertal burgeoning; perhaps even more significantly, it is a time of explosive brain development. In many ways, this period of change is no less dramatic than the miraculous emergence of a self-sufficient toddler straight out of babyhood. The teenager, neither a child nor an adult, finds himself in a totally new phase of life, requiring freedom and self-expression at the same time as boundaries, guidance, support and nurturing.

As parents, this new life stage often leaves us bewildered and baffled. We need to understand that teens aren't intentionally making bad choices or being careless. Many of their behavioural changes are due to significant reorganisation and 'rewiring' of the brain structures. They still need us to hug them and to truly listen to them, but they also need the space to express themselves. Do whatever you can to 'stay in the game,' urges Michael Grose, Australian parenting expert and author of eight books on the subject. He highlights the importance of staying connected and present as a parent through this challenging stage. He encourages us to take an interest in our teenagers' activities, drive them to places, talk to them about their friendships, about their life right now. Do whatever you can to keep connected and maintain a relationship.

1. TRANSFORMATION

Q: My sweet child has turned into something unrecognisable: What is going on here?

DAUGHTER: Why are you looking at me like that?

MUM: Like what?

DAUGHTER: I dunno, you are looking at me funny. And you embarrassed me in front of my friends by talking so loudly.

MUM: What do you mean?

DAUGHTER: Just like that. Whatever!

Doors slamming, raised voices, sulking and monosyllabic responses may be just some of the features you have experienced during the transformation of your cherubic child into a gangly teenager. Far more difficult, however, for teens than the physical changes of oily skin and pimples is the enormous brain development they undergo at this time. Teenagers endure (unbeknown to us or to them) changes as radical as when they were toddlers. Remember your excitement and praise at each major developmental milestone – clapping your hands every time your toddlers said a word or took their first shaky steps? As 14- or 15-year-olds reveal the by-products of a similar brain surge, challenging our assertions or expressing beliefs in conflict with our own, they are (sadly) unlikely to receive similar applause.

Also, cerebral and physiological growth spurts are accompanied by a new phenomenon – their peers' opinions matter more than their parents'. In the book aptly titled *Whatever!*, Gill Hines and Alison Baverstock explain that because teens fall awkwardly between two phases, namely childhood and adulthood, they are very different from either group: 'Their socialisation is different, their needs and wants are different and their bodies are different.' They are also trying to express their independence at the same time as being compelled to conform to their peer group. It's no wonder they're at risk for depression, anxiety, substance abuse and reckless behaviour. However, we can help our children through this stressful transition, with a few wise strategies.

WHAT TO DO:

- A combination of compassion, firm boundaries and open and honest communication is required.
- We need to expect change and, more importantly, expect our authority to be challenged.
- It's a good idea to give them space to take the steps.
- Keep those lines of communication wide open. It is a great relief and comfort for teens to know that they can express anything and not be judged.
- Respect their space and privacy.
- Don't stop hugging them.

2. BRAIN CHANGES

Q: Why doesn't my teenage son use his head clearly?

DAD: What were you thinking? Don't you think before you do anything?

SON: I just went over to Dean's house to hang out. I forgot I was supposed to meet you after soccer practice. It's not a big deal.

DAD: But we were worried. Why didn't you call? Don't you use your head?

SON: What are you talking about?

Science in the form of brain imaging has changed our understanding of adolescence. Recklessness, risk-taking and thoughtlessness, once thought to be products of pure self-centredness or raging hormones, are also the result of major brain development. Until fairly recently, we had no idea just how profound the brain changes during adolescence are. Research in the past decade has revealed that the brain undergoes significant reorganisation and suggests that teens aren't intentionally making bad choices or being careless.

Dramatic brain reconfiguration takes place in an area called the prefrontal cortex. This is the reasoning part of the brain, responsible for clear thinking and decision-making, and it undergoes a process often referred to as pruning. Areas of this critical brain structure are being rewired, making the brain more efficient. Some connections (called synapses) are literally whittled away or sloughed off, making way for new and stronger connections. The prefrontal cortex is also wired into the limbic system, the emotional part of brain that helps us make sense of the world and relate to others. The thinking processes are often thrown off course by activity triggered in the emotional part of the brain. A simple explanation for adolescent moodiness is that the thinking part of the brain has not yet developed to the point where it can rein in the intense reactions of the emotional brain. Dr Laura Kastner, clinical professor of psychiatry and behavioural sciences at the University of Washington, explains how neuroscientists characterise the risks inherent in teen years as a big engine, poor driving skills, faulty brakes and high-octane fuel: the big engine refers to the brash new push for autonomy, poor driving skills result from the reconstruction of the teens' prefrontal cortexes, faulty brakes describe the teens' lack of impulse control and high-octane gas refers to the intense emotions accompanying adolescents' hormonal changes.

WHAT TO DO:

- Understand that a lot of your teen's thoughtlessness is part of the building of a 'new' brain. This doesn't excuse poor conduct and insolence, but it does explain some sloppy behaviours and seemingly poor judgements.
- Use moments of calm and clarity, such as in the evening before bedtime, to engage with the teenager's thinking brain. This may be the optimum time to talk about, for example, the dangers of drunken driving and speeding, and the need to keep you abreast of their whereabouts.

3. BODY CHANGES

Q: How should I handle these dramatic physical changes in my teen?

MUM: Do you want to talk about periods?

DAUGHTER: No, not really, Mum.

MUM: Why don't you tell me what you know about periods?

DAUGHTER: Well, okay. Actually, I wanted to ask you something...

As they move from childhood into physical maturity, adolescents go through dramatic changes. We welcome these changes, but we also find them a little disturbing. Hormones, which are substances released by glands, signal the body to develop in certain ways. Puberty occurs when sex hormones signal the development of organs and systems related to sexual reproduction. Although many of the pubertal changes occur internally, there are also outward indications of the onset of sexual maturation. For girls, sexual maturation is marked by breast development and menarche, or the first menstrual period (on average, at between 10 and 15 years of age). For boys, it is marked by the production of viable sperm and the first ejaculation (on average, between the ages of 11 and 16), which is often indicated by nocturnal emissions, otherwise known as wet dreams. The sudden and rapid physical changes that they go through make adolescents very self-conscious and sensitive. Because body changes may not occur in a smooth, regular schedule, teens may go through awkward stages about their appearance and concomitant physical changes. The hormonal surges and fluctuations have a direct effect on emotions and thoughts too. Although male hormones kick in a little later than in girls, parents should still openly discuss sexuality and puberty with their sons as frankly as with their daughters.

WHAT TO DO:

- Address the issue of puberty with your young teens in an open and easy manner.
- Use a questioning approach, rather than dispensing lectures. Ask

them, for example, what they know about erections rather than giving them a lecture on the subject.

- Don't stop physical contact. Just because they are quite awkward about their bodies doesn't mean they need less physical contact.
- Dads sometimes feel reticent and nervous, and give up physical contact with their daughters. Do respect their boundaries, but don't stop hugging your daughters.
- Many dads may become physically more distant from their sons too. Both mums and dads should continue to show their teens a lot of physical affection even if they resist it somewhat.

COMMUNICATION

COMMUNICATING WITH TEENAGERS IS ONE of life's great contradictions. We want them to open up and speak to us. By contrast, they can think of nothing they would like to do less than have a heart-to-heart chat with their parents. 'If you are living with a teenager,' explains Australian parenting expert Michael Grose, 'you have probably noticed that they can be notoriously difficult to communicate with.' They mumble, they grunt, they speak in monosyllables and they become increasingly distant.

We genuinely want good communication with our children. We want them to feel that they can share ideas and opinions with us, and feel comfortable doing so. We want them to be able to discuss their problems with us. We want the daily exchange between us to be congenial. We wish for as little conflict as possible. The experts agree on good communication being the key to the best parenting. South African adolescent psychotherapist Serenne Kaplan emphasises that 'the core issue is reciprocal trust and mutual respect'. The trouble is that with teenagers effective communication is vastly different from what we think it should be. When we talk to our teens, there is so much that we want to convey as parents. We incessantly remind them to watch their language and not be rude; we feel the need to correct them frequently and point out when they just don't get it. This type of instruction comes naturally to us as parents. We have done it this way for more than a decade. It worked just fine when they were toddlers and preschoolers. It seemed to work really well through most of their primary-school years. But it just doesn't work any longer. This form of didactic guidance is in fact fairly useless with a teenager. 'Teenagers don't lose their ability to communicate, but their attention shifts away from parents and focuses like a laser beam onto their peers, particularly for those in the 14- to 16-year-old age groups,' explains Grose.

I often ask this question of teenagers: 'Why do you not like talking to your parents?' A frequent answer is: 'When we talk, they never shut up. They either don't listen to me, they lecture or they criticise. They don't really want to hear my point of view. So most of the time I don't even try.'

When a teenager initiates a conversation, unfortunately we almost always seem to add our agenda to the subject. We also feel the need to correct their point of view and we often object to the rude way in which they speak and the bad language they use. All of these, our agenda, our guidance and our objection to insolence, are most important and valid. But to encourage our teens to talk, we need to keep our opinions out of the way until a later stage.

Effective communication means that each person's needs, desires and opinions are considered. Teens need to know that their parents respect them even though we may not agree. Although they don't always show it, they appreciate it when we truly listen and pay attention to what they are saying in a non-judgemental manner.

4. 'I HEARD YOU!' . . . .

Q: How do we get teens to listen to us?

MUM: Ned, please could you take out the garbage?

SON: Yeah, okay.

MUM: Are you listening to me, Ned?

SON: Yeah, sure.

MUM: So, you'll take out the garbage?

SON: Yes.

MUM: Please go now?

SON: I'll do it in a minute.

MUM: No now!

SON: I heard you!

How often have your kids answered your second or third request to perform a simple task with 'I heard you!', but then felt no compulsion to actually do it?

OR CONSIDER THIS:

MUM: Leigh, please tidy up your incredibly messy room.

DAUGHTER: I will.

MUM: When will you do it?

DAUGHTER: Soon.

MUM: What does that mean?

DAUGHTER: Ah, Mum, please. I heard you!

The reality is that both Ned and Leigh are well-mannered and obliging young people. They are not defiant (well, generally not). If they were communicating with friends or school or university peers, they would not respond to a request with 'I heard you'.

So why is it that the response to a parent is so vastly different from the way they respond to peers or strangers? Dr Anthony Wolf, author of *I'd listen to my parents if they'd just shut up*, sheds light on this fascinating variance. He explains that adults and children have two distinctly different modes of behaviour, which he calls two different 'selves'. One he calls a domestic self, which just wants to unwind and be fed and will tolerate no stress. He calls this the 'baby self'. The domain of the baby self is the home, where it feels most comfortable and safe. In contrast, the 'mature self' functions at a much higher level. It goes into the world, is able to endure stress and delay gratification. This mature self has patience and self-control. Although we start life as a baby self, as we grow up, the mature self takes over most of our functioning. However, we all keep a part of our baby self, which emerges and seems to take over from time to time. Only in the baby self do we get the deep nurturing we need. Wolf explains that without a safe place for a baby self to rest, life would just be too difficult to endure.

So although it is infuriating when you hear 'Mum, where are my soccer boots?'; 'Mum, I can't find the TV remote'; 'Mum, I can't find my school jumper', this behaviour simply reveals that children need a place where they can fully be a child. And that place is at home, with us, their parents. There is no doubt that for most teenagers, the mature self is the major part of who they are, but the baby self comes to the fore very frequently as they swing between adult and infant. Rest assured that most teenagers will move out of this phase into perfectly good citizens as adults. How to tackle this problem is quite simple in theory but much more difficult in practice.

WHAT TO DO:

- Your teen needs a place where his baby self can emerge – and you want that place to be home.
- Do allow for the baby self to have a comfortable resting place within the confines of the home, but that doesn't mean tolerating insolence.
- There is no need to be overly concerned, as the mature self will certainly become the dominant part of the teenager with normal psychological development.

5. PARENT–TEEN CONFLICT . . . . . .

Q: Why is there so much conflict between teens and parents?

DAUGHTER: You said you don't like any of my friends.

MUM: I did not say I don't like any of your friends.

DAUGHTER: Yes, you did.

MUM: No, I didn't!

DAUGHTER: Yes, you did. You hate all my friends.

MUM: I do not hate all your friends; I dislike some of their behaviour.

DAUGHTER: There you go, you said it. Well I don't like your friends.

MUM: Do not bring my friends into it and don't be so rude.

DAUGHTER: I am not rude.

MUM: Yes, you are!

. . . .

There are a huge number of issues that may generate some sort of conflict between a parent and a teen. Most of the time, if we were able to disengage and move on, we could defuse many of these conflicts. The problem arises when we get locked into them and cannot shift. There is a clear explanation for this 'locked in conflict' state. We too as parents become our baby self when we are attacked or defied. Can you see this happening in the dialogue above? This is two baby selves in full-blown action and neither is prepared to back off and let go. If you have something you wish to say, stick to your original comment, plan or decision and then withdraw because your teenager certainly will not. Once they have heard your point, as the parent you must then back off. Serenne Kaplan urges parents to 'argue the point rather than the person and avoid harsh critical language and labelling but don't be afraid of your teen either'.

WHAT TO DO:

• Be aware that both you and your teenager have a 'baby self', whose domain is home where it feels most comfortable and safe, and a 'mature self'. Much of our conflict occurs when we are both in baby-self mode.

- As a parent, it is up to you to move into your adult rational state.
- When a baby self is not getting its own way it will go on and on, just like a two-year-old.
- The greatest skill we can learn as a parent is to disengage sooner rather than later in the conflict.

6. WHEN TO SHUT UP . . . .

Q: Are there times when I should just refrain from commenting and shut up?

MUM: Why are you so angry? What happened?

DAUGHTER: Caitlin's dad was late as usual to collect us from netball!

MUM: Well, now you can eat dinner and you've got some time to just relax.

DAUGHTER: I am so annoyed! It was so flippin frustrating!

MUM: I hope you weren't rude to Caitlin's dad.

DAUGHTER: Wow, Mum, I can't even talk to you! You always interrupt. You always have to try to pick on me.

. . . .

There are many times we need to shut up. That's correct: keep quiet as much as possible. Have I personally mastered this? Hell, no! But I am trying. It is one of the great lessons of parenting and has taken me almost a quarter of a century to begin to learn. If you were to ask any of my children whether I do the proverbial shutting up, they would say quite the opposite. They have a standard in-joke, which they find hilarious, but which I don't find particularly funny. As I am about to say something extremely important, all of them roll their eyes to the ceiling and one will exclaim, 'Now, which chapter of Mum's books is this?'. This has the effect of immediately shutting me up.

The reason we find it so hard to shut up is that we feel that if we don't correct our teen then and there, we miss the opportunity to teach her the right way. This feels like a loss of control, which it is. But that's exactly the point. Shutting up means letting go of the control that we may feel we need to exert. Of course, you need to use your discretion. You certainly won't shut up if he bashes your car, or she gets seriously drunk or you find marijuana in the house. But for everyday conversations and interactions, don't feel you have to use every opportunity to instruct. Let some of the issues go. Letting go of some control allows your teenager to talk and communicate further. If he doesn't feel judged, criticised or corrected then he may just begin sharing more than his three favourite words – 'fine', 'nothing' and 'later'.

WHAT TO DO:

- As difficult as it is to implement, learning to shut up when your teenager communicates with you will go a long way to enhancing your interactions and dialogue.
- Try to obstruct as little as possible.
- If we introduce our own agenda, we take his conversation in a new direction. It is far better to allow him to continue the flow by just listening, saying nothing or continuing the conversation in the direction it was originally heading.
- If you feel that there is something that needs to be commented on, it's best to wait until later. By stopping to correct him, the moment is gone and you may very well switch him off.
- Restraint and delay are very effective tools with teens.

7. BACKCHAT

Q: How do I deal with this backchat?

MUM: Just watch your mouth, Isabella! I don't like the way you are talking to me.

DAUGHTER: But you are rude to me!

MUM: You heard me now. Cut the backchat!

DAUGHTER: You should hear yourself!

Although it's not an easy thing to do, wait until a little later to address the issue. Allow the emotions on both sides to calm down. A common response to this is: 'If we don't respond immediately to this backchat, won't my teen feel as if she is getting away with it?' Anthony Wolf, author of *The secret of parenting*, says: 'Absolutely not. Just try my approach and see how much they hate for the power to rest in your hands.' They want the response. The backchat is to spark off your emotion, giving them a chance to manipulate you. When a child gives you backchat, you have two options – either to respond immediately or not to respond. If you respond to the backchat, chances are you will just get more of it.

WHAT TO DO:

- You may feel compelled to stop the backchat in its tracks. But by trying to stop it at the point of the exchange, you will probably just elicit further backchat.
- State what you need to say, do not respond to the backchat at all and if necessary, repeat your request calmly.
- The backchat will die down if there is nothing to feed off.
- Your teen will probably give far less backchat if you do not respond to it.
- Deal with it at a neutral moment, when the broader issue of disrespect can be addressed without emotional flooding (see page 150).

8. THE BEST WAY TO COMMUNICATE – LISTEN!

Q: What is the best way to communicate with my teen?

The best way to communicate with adolescents is counterintuitive: just listen. Truly listen. And if they still choose not to talk, let them know you are there to listen at any time and about anything. The notion that teens don't like to communicate with their parents is only partially true. They abhor being told what to do and they are not very good at taking criticism. (Neither are most adults, for that matter.) But they do like to be heard. Even the most introverted and monosyllabic teen appreciates being heard. It is the most basic part of being human. To a lesser or greater degree, we all want to share with someone what we feel and think. With teens, the people they choose to share with are not usually their parents, however. The reason is simple: at this stage, they would much rather share with their peers, explains Stephen Biddulph, child psychologist and author of bestseller *Raising boys* and *The new manhood*. It's a normal developmental experience, but it doesn't last forever. They eventually move out of adolescence into early adulthood and once again for the most part, value the relationship with their parents. Teens are also often betrayed or let down by a friend or partner and then need someone to turn to. But they will only share with you if they feel it's safe. We could take our relationship with our teens to the next level simply by being as non-judgemental and uncritical as possible while they are talking to us.

WHAT TO DO

- Listening does not necessarily mean you say nothing. The 'shutting up' part means withholding correction, criticism or rebuke.
- Being heard requires us to make eye contact and truly listen.
- For your teen to feel heard also means letting her know that you have understood what she has said, each step of the way. Psychotherapists use this technique all the time and it works. I am not suggesting we need to be using psychotherapy with our children,

but we do need to let them know they are being heard every step of the way. This involves some repetition of what they have said, instead of interjecting with what we think.

INSTEAD OF:

MUM: How was the party?

DAUGHTER: It was crappy.

MUM: Why was it crappy?

DAUGHTER: It just was.

MUM: Is something wrong? Did something happen at the party?

DAUGHTER: Casey is an f – – – ing bitch.

MUM: Don't use that language!

DAUGHTER: Oh to hell with it, you always lecture me!

HOW ABOUT?

MUM: How was the party?

DAUGHTER: It was crappy.

MUM: So it was really crappy?

DAUGHTER: It so was! And Casey is a real bitch.

MUM: So Casey was bitchy to you?

DAUGHTER: She embarrassed me in front of everyone.

MUM: You must have felt awful.

DAUGHTER: I did and I'm happy that I came home early.

MUM: It's a relief that you left the party?

DAUGHTER: Yip, anyway goodnight.

9. UNCOMMUNICATIVE TEENS

Q: Why is my teen so uncommunicative?

PARENT: How are you feeling?

TEEN: Grunt.

MOTHER: How was school?

DAUGHTER: Okay.

FATHER: Did you take out the garbage?

SON: I'll do it.

PARENT: What's news at school?

TEEN: Nothing.

. . . .

Since their earliest years, you have instilled in your kids great language skills through reading and spoken communication. So it is a bit disappointing to observe their verbal skills regress into monosyllables. But this is perfectly normal. It is also quite normal during adolescence for children to withdraw emotionally from their parents. Their peer group, which has its own language and set of rules, becomes their new forum for communication. Teens often disengage from parents if they sense we are not interested. They also withdraw when parents are overly critical. The secret is that 'communication with a teen doesn't necessarily mean talking', explain Michael Grose, author of *One step ahead: Great ideas for tired parents*. 'It can be hanging around and doing things together, perhaps playing a computer game, watching sport or driving to where they want to go.' There is little doubt that communication is the key to effectively parenting teenagers. Grose suggests a few helpful strategies to improve this relationship-building with your teen:

WHAT TO DO:

• Try to limit the amount of time they spend in their bedrooms.

Although they love their own space, and the time spent in their bedroom is part of an important developmental need for privacy, 'make sure they come out of their bedrooms for mealtimes and other opportunities to catch up,' emphasises Grose.

• 'Do take an interest in their interests.' Nurture something that you have in common, 'whether it's a shared love of music, sport or even shopping'. This is important relationship-building.

• 'Create the space for communication,' encourages Grose. You may need to create the environment where you and your teenager can talk. This may mean going out for a coffee or a meal alone.

• Be sensitive to their need for privacy.

• Truly listen to what they have to say.

10. 'I'LL DO IT LATER'

Q: Why is my teen's standard answer 'I'll do it later'?

MUM: Please tidy up the mess you left in the TV room.

SON: I'll do it.

MUM: Cameron, please go and tidy up that mess!

SON: I'll do it later.

. . . .

The problem with 'later' is that it usually means never. When your teen says that he will do it later, what he is generally thinking is if he puts it off for long enough, you will eventually give up on nagging him and he won't have to do it. He is probably also thinking that you will then do it for him. If we are honest with ourselves, most of us procrastinate at some time or another, but there is something innate about teens and procrastination. They are masters at it. It becomes so frustrating for parents that we tend to just give up. It becomes much easier to do it ourselves. 'Don't do this,' warns James Lehman, one of America's top child behavioural therapists and author of *Transform your child*. 'What you need to understand is that you are setting your child up to have a false sense of entitlement later on in life, a belief that the world owes them something.' It is a form of passive aggression that can be turned around, explains Lehman.

WHAT TO DO:

- The best time for later is now.
- If your teen's track record demonstrates that after saying 'later' he does get it done, then let up on him.
- Mostly, however, 'later' means never, so your prerogative is to make them do it now.
- Implement consequences for not responding to you. For example, if they don't bring their laundry to you, don't do their laundry.

11. SHARING WITH OTHER PARENTS (THE GOOD *AND* THE BAD)

Q: Why is it that all I hear from other parents is their children's successes?

PARENT NO. 1: What can I say? She is a natural swimmer.

PARENT NO. 2: We are very proud. This is his 10th goal this season.

PARENT NO. 3: Oh, academic success does come fairly easily. He doesn't do much studying.

PARENT NO. 4: She seems to have a natural talent for music.

It's understandable that as parents we all want to present our children in the best possible light. And when things aren't going well, we certainly don't want to reveal any of their problems or failures. Parents mistakenly absorb their kids' failures as their own and erroneously take on their offspring's achievements as well. In reality, most kids are not superstars even if their parents would have you believe so. Every child has some strengths and weaknesses. In a recent interview with Michael Grose, in which he spoke about some of his best advice on the subject of raising adolescents, he emphasised the 'drawing of strength from other parents'. Children today are very highly connected to each other; parents are not. 'You don't parent well in isolation,' he stresses. Grose encourages parents to connect through events at school and other organisations, and to speak to each other regarding children's boundaries and behaviours.

It would be liberating if we, too, could be a little more honest with each other. What emerges for many parents is the impression that no one else has any problems with their kids. Parents are reluctant to be open, honest and vulnerable. Obviously much of what goes on in our family lives is indeed private, but in reality even the best families have challenges and concerns. Every teenager, every relationship and every family has its obstacles, weaknesses and issues. Without having to expose ourselves totally, we could nevertheless draw strength from each other if we shared a little more than just our children's accomplishments.

- Without having to make yourself vulnerable, it is a good idea to begin to share your experiences of raising teenagers with like-minded parents.
- Become a good listener. You can provide support to fellow parents or friends going through a difficult time. No one is immune to many of the significant troubles experienced by teens. You never know when you may be in a similar situation.
- Remain modest about your kids' achievements. Although it is wonderful seeing them succeed, we should laud our children's qualities such as compassion, kindness and common decency with as much gusto as their successes.

12. TALKING TOUGH TOPICS

Q: How do I bring up difficult subjects with my teenager?

DAD: Did you see that your favourite British footballer has been charged with possible date rape?

TEEN: Are you serious?

DAD: Yes, it's on the news. Why don't you come and watch the headlines with me now?

We know that we need to begin a conversation with our teens about many very uncomfortable subjects. But how do you start to talk about safe sex, drug abuse or date rape? They are not merely awkward topics but these touchy subjects unfortunately may turn into parental lectures, which teens loathe. A great approach is to utilise the news, other media and what's current as a springboard to broaching such subjects with teens. This method takes the personal edge off the topic. A celebrity gets charged with rape; a football player is caught using cocaine; a teenager gets beaten into a coma at a party – are all opportunities to engage in a very meaningful conversation. But allow your teen to express his opinion on the matter before trying to jump in with the obvious moral message.

WHAT TO DO:

- Watch the news on television with your teen and use this as a springboard to ask his opinion, particularly on teen-related matters. The same applies to news sites on the computer or iPad.
- The nightly news or live talk-show programmes on relevant current issues provide an ideal opportunity for discussion and sharing your views on those tough topics.
- Reality TV shows, which teens are particularly fond of, provide countless moments for discussion and sharing.
- Listen more than you talk and you will discover that your teen will begin to want to hear more of your opinion.

- We do not need to try to be cool about every contentious issue. It is okay to have differing opinions, but do allow teenagers a chance to express their views even when they go against yours.
- Communicate your love as well as your expectations for decent conduct frequently and consistently, encourages Denise Wittmer, a recognised US author on parenting books, including *The parent's guide to raising a successful child*.

13. CONFRONTATION – 'WE NEED TO HAVE A TALK'.

Q: How do I best confront my teen about something he has done wrong?

DAD: We need to have a talk this evening, Sam.

SON: Oh come on, Dad, you look furious! What did I do now?

DAD: Have a shower and after dinner, we will talk.

. . . .

'Confronting our children is one of the less enjoyable aspects of parenting. Letting them know that they have done the wrong thing or that certain behaviours or attitudes are unacceptable is not pleasant,' explains Stephen Biddulph. He encourages us to 'give them some warning'. '"We need to have a talk" or "I need you and I to sit down after dinner, there is something we need to talk about" gives them time to process what it may be about and demonstrates a level of composure on your behalf,' recommends Biddulph.

What tends to happen with many parents is an eruption of anger, which leads to a most unproductive experience. You feel awful about losing it and you may lose the whole point of the discussion. Although it is okay for your teen to see you lose your composure, it is not the behaviour you want them to model. Make sure you have had a discussion with your partner or spouse before you confront the child and that you are in agreement. Biddulph also emphasises that fathers need to be actively involved in this aspect of parenting and not leave the tough stuff up to the mother.

WHAT TO DO:

- It is vital to choose a good moment to confront your teen. Do not begin as he arrives home, or as soon as he gets in the car.
- Don't confront him when you are furious. Wait until you feel calmer.
- If you land up shouting inappropriately, 'be sure to apologise after,' recommends Biddulph.

- Be cautious about how you speak and choose the content of what you have to say carefully.
- Say it straight and be direct. Don't attack your child, but be clear that you are angry at the behaviour.
- Be clear about the issues at hand. Once again reinforce the boundaries and stipulate your expectations for his behaviour.
- Try to end with a positive affirmation, such as: 'This is not the kind of behaviour I would expect from you. You are better than this.'

14. GENERATIONS Y AND Z

Q: How do parents cope with the whole new concept of Generations Y and Z?

MUM: What are you doing?

SON: The usual. I'm listening to music. Doing some homework, looking at Facebook. Why?… MIR.

MUM: What does MIR mean?

SON: Mum in room… Are you looking over my shoulder at what I'm texting?!

There has always been the proverbial generation gap. Parents were slated for not understanding their kids. But today's Gen Ys and Zs seem as though they're from another stratosphere. It has happened so fast that you could have children from two different generations in the same family. My three eldest are Gen Ys and the two youngest are Gen Zs, with me just making Gen X (or the tail end of the baby boomers).

Gen Y kids, born between 1980 and 1994, are known to be incredibly sophisticated and technology savvy. They have often grown up knowing it all, they've seen it all and been exposed to it all since early childhood, aided by the rapid expansion of the internet and cable TV channels. Having labelled them 'Generation Why', Eric Chester, speaker and author on the subject, explains that 'they are stimulus junkies, easily bored but also adept at multi-tasking, fast thinking, creative and tolerant of diversity'. They are often called the iGeneration or the MyPod generation. Dr Erica McWilliam of Queensland University, Australia, calls them the 'Yuk/Wow' generation. The media calls them Kippers (kids in parents' pockets eroding retirement savings). Technology is natural and normal for them. As 'netrepreneurs', they are smarter than Gen X (early/mid-1960s to 1980) and baby boomers (1946–1964), and they know it. They are into lifestyle, image and being entertained. They are always looking for the next opportunity or new job rather than promotion, as their parents did. Michael Grose calls them the zigzag generation, as they tend to change jobs frequently. He states that the average Australian 28-year-old will already have changed jobs three times. Some Gen Ys move back home after some years of freedom, after possibly having made some mistakes. 'But all is not lost,' he explains. 'There is a recovery period where many of them make a comeback in their mid-twenties.'

Generation Z children were born after 1995. They can multi-task, gather information quickly and make decisions faster. While we don't know as much about Gen Z as adults yet, we know a lot about the environment they are growing up in. Gen Z kids are growing up in a highly sophisticated media and computer environment, with digital communication and social networks, and are even more internet-savvy than their Gen Y forerunners. They have developed different communication styles from their parents and, ultimately, have experienced a radically different childhood from other generations. Unfortunately, many Gen Z kids are the products of significant affluence and helicopter parenting. They are learning far less in the form of life skills and more about being pushed to the limit.

WHAT TO DO:

- It is of great value to keep up to date with technology and social media so you can truly understand the digital environment that is so natural for our teens.
- Maintain your ethical and moral standards and expectations of your teens but make an effort to understand the differences between your generation and value system, and theirs.
- Although multi-tasking is natural, encourage activities and forms of engagement that require uni-tasking, for example a conversation without the presence of a cellphone, or a game of tennis.
- Gen Y and Z children are well known for wanting everything, now. Don't give in all the time. Train your Gen Ys and Zs in delaying gratification.
- Self-entitlement is also a strong feature of Gen Y and Z. Encourage gratitude and working towards goals and rewards.

MORALS, VALUES AND RULES

ALTHOUGH IT IS ESSENTIAL TO remain resolute with rules about safe behaviour in adolescence, be aware that many other parenting rules become redundant with time. It is absolutely appropriate at this stage for young adolescents to push for more autonomy and independence. This is often just a healthy expression of exploring their own emerging power, and may involve challenging many of the existing family rules.

Although we all have different parenting styles, most parents agree on the need to maintain a strong value system. I am personally far more rigorous when it comes to values and principles (social responsibility, compassion and decent manners, for instance) and far less rigorous about the rules governing conduct. Too many rules tend to create a punitive environment in which to raise a teenager. I believe with firm guidance and good role modelling, most teenagers will develop an internal locus of control and a strong sense of morality. However, even with the best parenting, you may encounter defiant adolescents who push the boundaries time and again.

Throughout this chapter, I have drawn advice from the leading adolescent experts worldwide on dealing with defiance, implementing basic safety rules, having confidence in your authority, learning to say no and attempting to inculcate a value system in teens. Involving your child in creating both the family rules and learning the consequences of breaking them may also help her understand and accept them.

15. DO TEENS NEED RULES?

Q: How does a parent enforce rules with a teenager?

DAD: Yes, you can take my car tonight – but you know the rules.

SON: I'm not drinking tonight at all, Dad.

DAD: And make sure none of your friends are drinking in the car either.

SON: I know the rules, Dad! If I'm going to be home later than expected, I'll call.

* * *

Every family's rules will be different. The standards you create will be influenced by your values and principles (see page 50), your situation, and your child's age and maturity. The regulational structures that may have worked for you through the early years of raising children are no longer appropriate or relevant for teens. At this stage, young people begin to explore their own power, and it is natural for them to push for more autonomy and independence. This can sometimes involve challenging the family rules. Involving your child in both setting the family rules and the consequences of breaking them, helps her understand and accept them. Many rules become redundant with time. Never touching an electrical socket is a most appropriate rule for toddlers, but no longer applies to older children. This obvious example serves to show, nevertheless, how we often retain unnecessary rules as a means of control. Boundaries are still important, however, and will help give your teenager a sense of security and let him know where he stands. One could categorise rules into three groups: do rules, don't rules and ground rules. With teens, keep the don't rules ('don't be rude') to a minimum. Do rules are easier to implement ('do speak politely'; 'do be kind'). And ground rules, the non-negotiables, which apply to all situations no matter what, such as rules about safe behaviour, are probably the most important elements for your teenager ('don't drink and drive'). These might include rules about alcohol use and safe sex.

Rules such as don't drink and drive, and values such as no lying or cheating should be unchangeable, cast in stone. But there are grey areas too. There is a certain degree of overlap between rules and values, reflected in the title of this book: body piercings may be absolutely forbidden and a non-negotiable for your teens. They were for me when my daughters were 12 or 13. This changed and by the time they were 16, I changed the rules. That's your prerogative as a parent. You make the rules, not because they are absolutely right or wrong. They are your rules because you believe in them and you as the parent implement them.

WHAT TO DO:

- Don't make unnecessary rules. Choose only the most important issues.
- Less is more. Establish a few clear, specific rules.
- Be willing to discuss and adjust the rules as your teenager gets older; be flexible.
- Revise your list of rules from time to time. For example, rules about spending time away from the family may need to be relaxed as privacy becomes more important for your teenager.

16. IMPLEMENTING RULES

Q: How do I implement rules with my adolescent?

MUM: Where are you going?

DAUGHTER: I'm not sure.

MUM: I need to know where you're going before you leave.

DAUGHTER: None of my friends have to tell their parents where they're going.

Teens are adept at making their parents feel like they are the only weird ones who need to have rules. A family is a unit that thrives on structure and rules. Guidelines may be a better term than rules, which may sound too authoritarian. Whatever we call them, though, we all need guiding principles and rules to live by – no one more so than a teenager. 'The two key factors are to choose your rules, albeit allowing for some flexibility and then ensure you maintain them', encourages psychotherapist Serenne Kaplan. Many issues within a family can be negotiable, but there are a few that are not. Rules will vary depending on the values of the family and the type and age of the teenager.

Knowing your teenager's whereabouts is a basic requirement. The issues that usually require a set of guidelines are places where teens may and may not go, the time they should be back home (curfews), housework and homework. Other issues, such as honesty, compassion and kindness, are more accurately described as values. But these too become a family's set of rules to live by. Since early childhood, my children have internalised honesty as a core family principle. They know this is a far more important 'rule' than getting home on time. When it comes to implementing rules, open communication and discussions about concerns of parents and teens help build compliance.

WHAT TO DO:

- Know your kids' whereabouts. This should be one of the non-negotiable rules. You are entitled to answers to these questions:
  - » Where are you going?

>> Who are you going with?
>> How are you getting there and back?
>> When will you be home?

- When setting a rule, remain calm and be clear.
- Even out differences of opinion with your partner or spouse before setting down a guideline. Be on the same page from the start.
- Do not make decisions in a vacuum. Do some research by discussing with other parents, and possibly school counsellors, what is age appropriate.
- Discuss the policies with your teenager and explain how you came to your decisions. Truly listen to their point of view.
- Be flexible and communicative, but be clear about non-negotiables.
- Don't expect teenagers to be pleased about some of the rules.
- Renegotiate and open the discussion every so often.

17. FAMILY VALUES

Q: Are family values different from rules?

SON: You know, Dad, all the boys pass round cheat notes during a class test. Do you think that is really such a bad thing?

DAD: Steve, I do think it's a really bad thing. I think any kind of deceit that includes lying and cheating is very serious. It goes against basic conduct. I would rather you failed the test every time than ever cheat.

What is arguably more important than rules is a set of unchanging internal family values. These are not age or stage dependent, but the very fabric of your family. Their significance lies in their potential to become the moral fibre of your children. You cannot enforce values, you can only live them. When parents live their values, their children will often imbibe these principles. Adolescents, however, will often challenge parents' values and beliefs, but this is a healthy developmental stage. They may also discard some of them, but later, as adults, they will probably revisit these values.

All families have some set of internal rules. As parents, we may think that these principles are well understood, but they may become blurred for a restless adolescent.

Without an articulated set of family values, teenagers have no yardstick against which to measure any of their behaviours, good, bad or rebellious.

To share an example, let's take stealing and lying. You will agree with me that as a fundamental value all families would oppose these. Well, how far does your family value extend? I have always expressed to my children that cheating in a test is the same as stealing or lying. It may not feel as if they are breaking a serious law peeking over their friend's shoulder and copying in a test. My message to my children has always been that I would prefer them to fail every test than cheat even once. They know that in the same way that compassion and honesty are core values, cheating, lying or any form of deceit goes against our family values. There are many parents who may convey the message to their children that it is perhaps okay to claim a little higher from insurance, tell a white lie or do a really good deal by taking advantage of some loophole or bending the rules ever so slightly. Our children observe and absorb the morals and ethics of our adult behaviour. Be clear to your children that integrity is important to you, but, more importantly, uphold these values in your behaviour if you expect the same from them.

Home is the place we can counter some of the messages that may be imparted to children by society, such as winning at any cost. We may set the bar high in terms of what we expect of our children regarding compassion towards others, loyalty, ethical conduct and social responsibility. But we need to set the bar much higher for ourselves first.

WHAT TO DO:

- Be clear about your own values.
- Articulate your values to your teens, even if they choose to openly reject them.
- It is a normal feature of development, and often healthy adolescent behaviour, to reject the family's value system.
- Allow your teen to verbalise and challenge your value system.
- Set the bar high for ethical and moral conduct for your children and more so for yourself.

18. A PARENT'S INFLUENCE

Q: How can we as parents have any influence over our teens?

SON: You don't trust me!

MUM: It's not that. I just want to know where you will be tonight.

SON: You don't give me any freedom.

. . . .

'Trust and freedom,' according to Australian adolescent expert and author of eight books Michael Grose, 'need to be earned.' He believes that teens are not necessarily entitled to freedom just by reaching adolescence. They need to prove that they are worthy of it. It is very testing to maintain our parental authority in this age of the internet, social media and instant communication. In the past, the parent was the gatekeeper. Our parents would answer the phone and hear the voice of our friends; they would open the door when a boyfriend came to visit. It was so much easier for them to have an idea of what was going on in our lives.

Today it is much more difficult to know what is happening in our teenagers' lives. We don't even hear the music that our kids are listening to as they navigate the world with earphones and iPods. They are in a very private world, interconnected to others in ways that are harder to monitor. But all is not lost. 'I take an optimistic view on today's kids,' Grose explained to me. He compares the internet to the shopping malls of the past. Our parents would drop us at the mall for a few hours but we still had the freedom to go into shops, movie theatres and game arcades. With guidance, good role modelling and a set of values, we could choose to engage in untoward behaviour or not. The same is still true today. Parents lack confidence in their influence and their ability to stand their ground. Now more than ever we can reclaim our influence and give our kids tremendous strength. Providing our children with guidance and social and moral skills allows them to adapt to the challenges of today.

WHAT TO DO:

- 'Have confidence in your authority,' encourages Grose, and stand your ground. Remember that you are the parent.
- You have several years to influence your teenage children. Take the time to get it right.
- Your teen needs to earn more freedom by demonstrating responsible behaviour. The greater the responsibility shown, the more freedom can be given.
- Reclaim your personal power and influence – you are the parent. This does not mean controlling behaviour but a strong, confident parent is necessary for your adolescent's full development.

19. SAYING NO

Q: Why do I find it so difficult to say no?

MUM: Jessie, no! I said no and I am not going to change my mind.

DAUGHTER: But, Mum, the whole crowd is going. I'll be the only one not going. I can't not go, Mum. It's not fair!

MUM: What do I have to do to make you understand that no means no?

DAUGHTER: You have to say yes!

Saying no to teenagers is certainly one of the most difficult things to do, mainly because they have such smart and manipulative ways to persuade you otherwise. Once you have said no, it doesn't really matter what you subsequently say, because all that matters is whether you mean no or not. Decide before delivering your categorical no that you are sure. Then say no; give a clear and very simple explanation, and do not engage further. In reality, the more reasons you try to give, the more strategies they seem to manage to apply to change your mind. They are not interested in appreciating your reasons for the no. Each reason is a starting point for an argument and as far as teens are concerned, all nos are unfair.

Don't expect a harmonious outcome after delivering your no. If it is something you feel strongly about, stick to it. But be careful not to deliver too many unnecessary nos. There are many instances when you can be flexible and negotiable. 'If you want to understand your teenager, subtract twelve years,' explains Michael Grose. Your 14-year-old is not unlike a two-year-old in many ways, including pushing boundaries, taking risks, craving independence and mostly in his inability to take no for an answer.

WHAT TO DO:

- Say no as little as possible.
- Say no when necessary and mean it.

- Reach a decision with your spouse in private before delivering the no and maintain a common front.
- Listen to your teen and show respect for his viewpoint.
- It is a good idea to give a simple, clear reason for your no, although it will usually be rejected.
- Keep cool. There is no doubt your teen will pull out all the stops to bait you or accuse you of being unfair.
- Once you have stated your case, move away.
- Use no sparingly and only for important issues. If you find yourself saying no to most issues all the time, you might be setting up a punitive parenting pattern that could backfire.

20. CONSEQUENCES

Q: How do I get my teenage son to learn from his mistakes?

DAD: I allowed you to take my car, trusting you would drive responsibly.

SON: I know, Dad, but these things happen.

DAD: They don't just happen, you were speeding!

SON: I am sorry but what can you do? I wasn't concentrating on the speed limit.

DAD: You will pay the speeding fine out of your money and you will not be driving my car at all for the next three months.

Teenagers don't learn much from parents' warnings or lecturing. They learn best by making a mistake and having to endure the consequence. The reason they remember the lessons when there are consequences is that they are then able to work it out for themselves. A consequence is best learnt if the parent of a teenager simply enforces the consequence but doesn't get emotionally or physically involved in it. When kids have developed to adolescence, rewards and punishments just don't seem to work very well any longer. They may work temporarily. Things like grounding and taking away access to cellphones and the internet are not particularly effective. 'You can't *punish* kids into acceptable behaviour – it just doesn't work that way,' explains James Lehman, adolescent therapist. We often wonder why teenagers behave irresponsibly. The reason is that as they straddle the corridor between childhood and adulthood they *are* irresponsible. And they cannot mature or become responsible until they deal with the consequences of their behaviour each time they falter. It is a cycle that needs to occur over and over before a teen comes to full maturity.

WHAT TO DO:

- Keep calm. Try to keep your anger at bay as best you can.

- 'I'm disappointed in you'-type statements don't seem to have much value or impact.
- The intention with consequences is to make the teen angry at himself for knowingly doing something dangerous or foolish.
- Let your teen know well in advance what the consequences of misconduct or ignoring requests are. Communicate them clearly.
- Avoid implementing arbitrary and angry rules and consequences after the event.
- If consequences have not been part of your parenting strategy until now, let your teen know that you are making changes and give them time to adjust to this new approach by explaining clearly the consequences.

21. BUT ALL THE OTHER PARENTS LET THEM! . . . .

Q: How do you say no to your teen when 'all the other parents let them'?

MOTHER: Ned, please hurry up and choose the video you want to watch with your friends at the sleepover.

SON: I can't find anything; the only one that my friends want to watch is *Kill Bill*.

MOTHER: I've told you no already. It is extremely violent and has an age restriction of over 16.

SON: All the other boys' parents let them watch whatever they want!

. . . .

This statement must be the most popular of all teenage battle cries. Every one of my five children has used this line at one time or another. It is popular because it is so effective. It hits parents right where they are vulnerable and is manipulative because if you are not utterly convinced of your decision, you can be easily swayed. We don't want to be the difficult and weird parents. This is particularly true if your kid is not completely comfortable within the peer group. You may feel that your 'hard line' is making it even more difficult for him to fit in. And even if he is comfortable in his group of friends, it can still be tricky. Michael Grose calls this 'teens ganging up on their parents'. He explains that we often learn about this sneaky trick with our first child and become wiser with the next. But he highlights a very interesting notion: 'Kids are more highly connected to each other, whereas parents are not.' Constantly interconnected via Facebook and instant messages, they keep checking with one another to sell the same story to their parents. 'You don't parent well in isolation,' explains Grose. He advises parents to do the same – stay in frequent contact and share information; this allows parents to draw strength from one other.

WHAT TO DO:

- Choose your battles. Be clear about issues that are genuinely not negotiable and then stand your ground. But do try to be flexible with other, more negotiable, issues.

- Network with other parents, particularly those of your child's peer group.
- Keep in communication with these parents, check in with them and draw strength from this network. Grose suggests this as a strategy and offers the suggestion to take advantage of schools to create social opportunities for parents to connect without their teens.
- If you are not on the 'same page' as other teens' parents, be resolved about the issues you feel strongly about. It takes courage to parent effectively.

22. IT'S NOT FAIR!

Q: How do you deal with 'it's not fair'?

SON: But why not?

MOTHER: Because it's violent and because I said so.

SON: It is so not fair! You let the girls watch whatever they want.

MOTHER: They are 21 years old.

SON: And you always let Alex watch anything.

MOTHER: No I don't.

SON: You so do! And Gabe said he used to watch scary movies with Dad when he was younger.

MOTHER: He did not.

SON: It's not fair! It is sooo not fair!

. . . .

When it comes to the 'not fair' debate, no reasoning about the whys and why nots will ever satisfy a teenager. When young children ask why and why not, you are encouraged to give as much information and as many answers as possible to expand their knowledge, understanding and curiosity. Giving answers to teens is wide of the mark! Absolutely no answer will put the lid on it. The most effective way to deal with the 'it's not fair' and 'tell me why not' challenge is to end the conversation there and then, and move away. Disengage. Even though it may not be over. This is another one of the 'teen speak' comments that is extremely effective as it hits at our core. Our entire world view is built on fairness. We want life to be fair for us and for them. They know this and will often play you off against the other siblings. There is no way that a parent can win a fair or unfair debate with a teenager. In their minds, if you say no it is unfair. Dr Anthony Wolf, author of *It's not fair, Jeremy Spencer's parents let him stay up all night*, says: 'It is excellent to listen to your teen. But engage in a true fairness debate? Avoid that at all costs.'

WHAT TO DO:

- You cannot debate 'it's not fair' – you cannot satisfy the question or win the debate. Say no, disengage and then move away.
- Teenagers have an arsenal of phrases designed to manipulate their parents. Before you say no to a request, be sure that you really mean it and then stick to your guns.

23. UNITED WE STAND

Q: What if we as parents disagree with each other on discipline and boundaries?

DAD: I have already stated my viewpoint. There is no way I will allow you to take the car again.

SON: That is so unfair!

MUM: Yes, Bob, you are being a bit unfair.

SON: See, Dad, Mum says it's okay, and I won't damage the car this time.

The experts all agree that it is important for parents to present a united front when dealing with discipline issues and establishing boundaries. Jim Fay and Foster Cline, authors of *Parenting teens with love and logic*, suggest a rule of thumb: 'The more irresponsible the teen, the more important it is for the parents to agree on the discipline they use.' They suggest that the less problematic the teen, the more leeway the parents have to openly present different ideas. With a very difficult child, they emphasise that 'the united front must be absolute, with no cracks in it: This is where we stand. Period.' If you are arguing between yourselves about an issue, it will be impossible for you to enforce any type of boundary or internal ethical principle. You will just create an environment in which your child will be manipulative, playing off one parent against the other.

WHAT TO DO:

- Come to an agreement with your partner before you address the issue with your child. Create a united team.
- Even if you have different standpoints on an issue, most of the time you will be able to reach some middle ground before discussing it with your teen.
- If you reach an impasse, it might be worth seeking help from a professional counsellor or therapist, particularly if it is a serious issue.

24. CURFEWS

Q: What are the guidelines for implementing curfews?

DAD: What time will you be home?

DAUGHTER: Around midnight.

DAD: Will you let us know if there's a problem or if you think you will be home later?

DAUGHTER: I will, Dad.

There are many different approaches to teenage curfews. I personally don't believe imposed curfews are valuable. The teens who do need such directives generally defy the curfew and those who don't need them just don't need them. 'The real world doesn't have curfews,' explains Foster Cline, psychiatrist and author of eight parenting books. 'And if we are raising our teens to live in the real world, we shouldn't have curfews either.' The best way to deal with curfews is to negotiate and agree on a reasonable time to return home. Of course, some basic ground rules are needed first. You are entitled to ask and get straight answers to these questions: Where are you going? Who are you going with? How are you getting there and back, and when will you be home? The issue of negotiating is not to lessen your power as a parent, it is simply to come to a reasonable agreement. The reason for the big deal made about curfews is simply that parents worry. We worry about our children's personal safety, and when they are not home when expected, we worry more. So the issue is not the curfew per se, it is knowing where your child is and what time she is expected home. Being informed that they will be a bit later than expected is the main issue. Parents react in this situation first by being afraid and then becoming angry. However, all that the teen perceives is the anger, not the real parental concern.

WHAT TO DO:

- A good family rule to establish in place of curfews is always knowing your teen's whereabouts and expected time to be back home.

- You need to be able to contact your children, and they you, in case of an emergency.
- Explain to your teen that setting a time to return by is not a question of control and punitive action. The motive is that you are concerned about their wellbeing – that is the only reason you need to know their whereabouts.
- Insist on answers to these four questions (see 'Implementing rules' on page 48):
  » Where are you going?
  » Who are you going with?
  » How are you getting there and back home?
  » When will you be home?
- If they do not give you answers to these questions, or mislead you, you should not necessarily impose a curfew, but they should be made to feel the consequences of their actions, for example by preventing them using the car.

25. PARTIES

Q: What should I be concerned about with regard to teenage parties?

SON: None of my friends have their parents at home when they have a party.

DAD: I don't intend to be at the party – but I will be home. The safety of all the guests is my responsibility.

SON: I'm not a baby. I don't need you spying.

DAD: I will certainly not be spying. I will stay out of the way. So you've got a choice.

One frequently reads horror stories about brawls, drunkenness, sexual activity and lack of supervision at teenage parties. The reality is that the issues associated with a typical teenage party traverse all the major adolescent territories. Teenagers have always had parties and always will. You will find risky behaviour, binge drinking and sexual exploration; you will find lonely individuals trying to fit in; you will also find teens who hate parties; you will have children lying and defying parents who forbid them to go to a party; you will hear the words, 'It's not fair, all the other kids' parents let them go!'

There is clearly no prescriptive expert approach when it comes to parties. But you can apply some of the common-sense strategies already discussed in other sections. And remember, not all parties are bad. They are occasions for teens to socialise and satisfy the human need for interaction with others. As Michael Grose suggests (see 'Risk-taking: Sex, drugs and rock 'n' roll' on page 193), 'stay in the game' with your teens. With regard to parties, this means driving them to the party, knowing whose party it is and arranging a pickup time (particularly with younger teens). Check with other parents as to whether there may be anything untoward to be concerned about. Often another parent may know that there will be no parental supervision at a particular party, for example, or that marijuana was used at a party of the same family's older child. If you choose to forbid your child to go, stick to your decision (see 'Saying no' on page 54). If your child hosts a party, you must understand that you are responsible for the guests' safety and it is necessary to have adult supervision at all times (albeit discreet and in the background).

(see 'Saying no' on page 54)

WHAT TO DO:

- Establish ground rules about parties in general.
- If you have agreed for your teen to host a party, work out the ground rules with him before the party is announced.
- Never give an order that you cannot enforce. This often backfires. Rather than saying, 'I forbid you to hold a party while we are away', it is more effective to state: 'I hope you will avoid having parties while we are away because you know you will be paying for all the damage to the property out of your allowance.'
- Supervision of parties by responsible adults is necessary, even though your kids may not agree.
- Whatever the age of your teen, it is reasonable to insist that you will be present at home but out of the way: you have a responsibility to ensure the supervision and safety of those attending.
- Have confidence in your authority as the parent and stand your ground.

26. APPEARANCES

Q: Why does my teen have to dress so weirdly?

MUM: What are you wearing?

DAUGHTER: What do you mean?

MUM: What is that?

DAUGHTER: It's a dress! What's wrong with it?

Of all the issues that emerge during adolescence, this is probably one that we would do well to ignore. Teenagers express their independence and autonomy in many ways. They have a deep need either to fit in with the crowd or to stand out from the crowd. Sometimes they do both at the same time. Nowhere is this urge more evident than in their appearance. Their appearance is probably one of the most harmless of these expressions, and it is best not to make a fuss – consider it one less adolescent battle for parents to have to fight.

What appears to us as totally off-the-wall fashion usually turns out to be what everyone else is also wearing. The teenage years are a time young people establish their identity, and clothing and appearance help them in this formation of a self. Hairstyles in particular have always been a strong statement of the young, from afros and long hair in the sixties to punk-rock cuts in the seventies and mohawks of the nineties. Body piercings (see page 69) are an extension of this desire to look cool and make a statement. Depending on the age of your teens and your stance on piercings, this may, however, be a more complex issue than hairstyles and clothes.

WHAT TO DO:

- Try to say something complimentary as long as you aren't actually lying – especially if this week's haircut or dress style is just slightly better than last week's.
- If there is nothing positive to say about your teen's appearance, then say nothing.

- Humour is a good approach, as long as he thinks it's funny and can take a joke.
- Try to avoid turning your views on appearance into a control issue. When possible let it go.
- If your child's appearance is offensive, then it is a good idea to ensure you do not pay for clothes and hairstyles that you really abhor.

27. BODY PIERCINGS AND TATTOOS

Q: What should parents do about body piercing and tattoos?

SON: I don't understand why you have a problem. It's no big deal!

MUM: I personally don't like it at all. I am not saying it is forbidden forever. But not now. We can discuss it again in a year or two. But my answer right now is no.

SON: You are just being mean.

Has your child gone from clean cut to pierced and tattooed? If so, you're definitely not alone. Body piercing has become a huge trend among teens and while they think it's just a cool thing and a form of self-expression, parents are concerned about it. As you will have gleaned from the introduction to this book, I personally shifted from being totally opposed to all piercings to accepting what I think are the benign forms of this trend. Although I tolerate belly rings and nose piercings, I can't bear tongue rings and abhor the idea of nipple and genital piercings.

Just a generation ago, many parents wouldn't allow their daughters to have their ears pierced, and a boy with an earring was labelled rebellious or gay. I clearly remember almost 30 years ago a friend of mine from medical school who asked his conservative father for permission to have his ear pierced. Expecting a tirade of anger, he was astonished when his dad replied extremely calmly, 'Certainly. Just make sure you get contact lenses at the same time, because you will have nowhere to hang your glasses – I will cut off your ear!' Today there has been a shift in society's acceptance of piercings, but it is still a very personal decision as to what you will allow. Tattoos may have become more acceptable, but my personal opinion is that they are worse than piercings. At least the ring can be removed and the hole will close up.

Age appropriateness is also important. At 13 it was out of the question for my daughters to have a navel or nose ring, but when they reached 16 I felt less opposed. One has to ask the question, 'What does this situation at this age and stage of my child's development require of me?' advises Michael Grose. Over and above your personal objections, the consequences of body piercing can be serious from a health perspective. The most common problem is infection at the site of the piercing with the formation of pus and swelling, and the possibility of an abscess forming. Oral piercings have a particularly high rate of complications. Although rare, more serious infections – such as hepatitis B and C, HIV and tetanus – can occur, particularly as a result of unsanitised needles and seedy tattoo parlours. Blood-borne disease, such as endocarditis, which affects heart valves, can occur in children with underlying known or unknown heart conditions.

WHAT TO DO:

- Don't fight over this issue; try to communicate calmly.
- Attempt to listen to her view and why she wants a piercing.
- If she asks for permission, ask her to wait for a while before you revert to the discussion at a later stage – you need time to consider this.
- If you are willing to agree, set out rules from the outset as to what you are prepared to permit, such as earrings, a nose ring or navel ring, but no other body parts and no tattoos, for example.
- If you are willing to allow tattoos, that is your decision but make it clear that they are irreversible.
- Let your child know that if she violates your ruling and goes behind your back, there will be consequences. Take away privileges such as driving or paying for her cellphone.
- Equip your child with the following medical information: a nipple ring can cause severe scarring and damage, and she may never breastfeed; tongue piercings can become seriously infected; genital piercings are the worst and can result in bacterial infections, nerve damage and heavy scarring.
- Remember you are the parent: stand your ground. It's okay to be unpopular.

28. HOMEWORK

Q: How should I get my child to take his homework more seriously?

MUM: Don't you guys have homework that you need to complete?

SON: I don't have any homework.

DAUGHTER: I finished my homework at school.

SON: I'll do it later.

For as long as there is a school system as we know it, there will always be homework. Too much homework is the constant grumble of many kids and although some teens have a natural sense of responsibility when it comes to completing homework and assignments, most find ways to resist it or procrastinate. Research demonstrates that there is sometimes a gender disparity, in that girls on the whole are far more conscientious than boys.

I certainly agree with adolescent psychologist Dr Michael Carr-Gregg, who recommends that parents should begin to wind down helping their children with school work sooner rather than later. In an Australian internet survey of 1 178 primary-school children, Carr-Gregg found that 22 per cent said their parents did the homework for them. Although supervision is required in junior school and guidance is needed from time to time in earlier primary-school years, by the time your children are in senior primary, and certainly high school, parental involvement should be minimal.

My children often complained that I was an unkind mum who wouldn't do their school projects for them or with them. They would often describe how Daniel or Emma got an A+ on their project because their mums and dads were amazing at art and really helped. Are such parents really proud of their A grade for a Grade 8 project? What is being achieved? Are they competing with other parents or other kids? I am not advocating zero assistance: there are certain aspects of homework in which we should assist. Whenever my children have finished studying for a test and want me to question them, I will take as much time as needed. Similarly, if they are stuck on a particular query, I will help if I can.

The many reasons for teenagers not completing their homework may include sheer laziness, defiance, lack of motivation or genuine learning problems, so it is important to determine the underlying issues. For many years, adolescent specialists have argued the point on whether to let children fail and experience what happens when they do not do their work. As with so many other factors regarding adolescent behaviour, the correct approach is to back off and allow them to suffer the consequences. Anthony Wolf mentions in his books that this was his approach until recently. He states that he now believes that when kids cannot get their act together with school and homework, parents most definitely do need to be involved. He describes that trying to motivate them through incentives and 'bribes' just does not work in the long run. He explains that although you cannot force them into doing homework, you can structure the environment to create the greatest likelihood that the work will get done. He advises a system that is in fact used in the best boarding schools. For a set period per day (the times can be varied on different days) there should be a study time, possibly an hour to two, depending on the child's age. The rules are that there is nothing else they are allowed to do during this time: no TV, no Facebook, no games, no cellphone. It is important that a parent is home during this time. Kids may stare into space during this study session, but eventually most do begin to use this time to complete homework. If you stick with this plan, they will get used to it and get better at completing homework.

WHAT TO DO:

- Do not hover over high-school children during their homework – leave them to get on with it.
- However, if they cannot get homework and school work done, and are failing or underachieving, do step in, be firm, create structures and allow a little bit of stress.

THE FAMILY

THE FAMILY STRUCTURE IS A microcosm of the world. It is where our children learn about relationships, about conflict and harmony, about compromise and cooperation. But it is also a buffer zone away from the harshness and pain of the outside world. Ideally, the family is a comfort zone and a place where our children can be themselves, warts and all. Of course the family can also be a place of great dysfunction and damage. But if you are reading this book, this is unlikely, as you are obviously a responsible parent wanting the best for your teen.

This chapter provides you with an opportunity to explore your style of parenting, whether it be helicopter hovering or the tiger-parent style. It provides some expert insights and strategies to deal with the ever-present issue of sibling rivalry, mother's guilt, trying not to screw them up, owning the problem, building common interests with your teen and understanding the gender divide.

29. PARENTAL INVOLVEMENT ....

Q: Just how involved in my teen's life should I be?

DAUGHTER: Mum, I'm going to the mall for a short while to check out shoes for the dance.

MUM: I'll come with you to help you choose.

DAUGHTER: No, it's okay, I'm happy to go on my own.

MUM: Are you sure? I'd like to come.

DAUGHTER: Yeah, I am sure.

. . . .

How involved should we be? There are probably as many answers to this question as there are parents in the world. Your parenting style is drawn from your own childhood, your value system, your philosophy on life and, of course, your personality. Are you an anxious or calm person? Are you rigid or lenient? An introvert or outgoing? All these factors, and many others, will affect your approach. Some parents, for example, use every type of online parent control to monitor their child's internet activity, whereas others wouldn't consider it. Some will routinely snoop around and try to determine exactly what their kids are doing, while others wouldn't bother unless they stumbled upon some misbehaviour. I fall into the latter category, but there is no right approach. Whether you are hyper-vigilant or more lenient, Dr Antony Wolf, Boston-based clinical psychologist and author of five parenting books, suggests that a good guideline to follow is your teenager's track record.

If your 15-year-old son regularly pushes the limits and has been in trouble frequently, you will want to watch him and monitor risky situations. On the other hand, if he is a compliant kid who has not caused any problems, there is no need for major surveillance. Then again, there are instances where parents are either in denial of their child's waywardness or have no idea what is happening. Most teens fit somewhere in the middle ground – neither serious offenders nor models of perfect behaviour. It is best to stay alert and have a basic level of awareness without constantly hovering over their affairs.

- Teens need space. Allow them freedom away from you.
- Give them a degree of independence, which should be age-appropriate, so allow more independence as they get older, but stay observant.
- Remain available to be contacted when they need assistance.
- Insist on knowing the answers to these four questions (see also 'Implementing rules' on page 48):
  » Where are you going?
  » Who are you going with?
  » How are you getting there and back?
  » When will you be home?
- If you have the challenge of a defiant child, then you will need to monitor him much more closely and get professional advice or intervention if necessary.
- If you are not sure what's happening, consult teachers, school mentors or other parents.
- Trust your intuition if you suspect something is not right.

30. SIBLING CONFLICT

Q: How should I handle my teenagers' constant bickering?

SON 1: Mum, don't listen to him. That's not what happened.

SON 2: He is such a liar. It's not fair. You always believe him!

MOTHER: Well, what happened?

SON 1: He started with me, as always. He won't shut up.

SON 2: You see, you always believe him.

For most parents, a major source of annoyance is constant sibling squabbles. Sibling rivalry is something that even the best of families will encounter. Life in general, and families in particular, are full of rivalry, and the teenage years are no exception.

Although one of the accepted golden rules of parenting is to keep out of sibling clashes at all times, it is very tempting as a parent to jump in and try to finish it off. But this does more harm than good. Although we hate to see our children fighting, sibling rivalry is a way for teenagers to learn appropriate ways of getting along with others. It gives them a chance to experiment and deal with situations they may encounter with others outside of their family. The only exception to non-intervention is when they resort to physical conflict. This is particularly important with teens, who now have the ability to cause injury. The 'no physical contact' rule should be inculcated as a non-negotiable family code from early childhood. During a teenagers' quarrel you cannot possibly try to listen to each child's perspective. Your involvement achieves only one thing: each child tries to get you on their side. 'It's much better not to listen,' advises Dr Anthony Wolf. 'Listening only fuels the fire. It's much better to throw the responsibility of working out a solution back on them,' he explains.

WHAT TO DO:

- Do not get involved in or try to mediate your teens' arguments unless they are physically hurting each other.

- Establish the rules regarding sibling conflict. The most important rule to set is zero tolerance of physical violence. Make it clear to your teens that physical violence is never allowed. Establish consequences for physical violence long before it gets the chance to erupt.
- Create a forum for teens to express their grievances and gripes. This may be after dinner or at a neutral and calm time, when they have the opportunity to be heard by you and their siblings.
- Spending a little one-on-one time with each child also provides an opportunity for them to be heard.

31. MOTHER'S GUILT: IT'S ALL MY FAULT!

Q: Why do I often feel guilty about my parenting?

MUM: I shouldn't go to the gym, I should be at home with my kids now.

MUM: If it weren't for my long work hours, Tom wouldn't have landed up smoking weed.

MUM: If I had been home at the time, that would never have happened.

Nearly all mothers experience some form of guilt, whether it's a feeling that they aren't doing enough for their children, a sense of guilt over choosing to do something for themselves without their kids or feeling guilty when things go wrong. The 25 years of parenting my five children have been peppered with moments of mother's guilt: weaning too soon; leaving a tiny infant so I could complete my medical internship; working throughout my child-rearing years; travelling too much. And then having a premature and sick baby must have been my fault too?

Society puts a lot of pressure on women to do what is supposedly right for the family. Gail Kauranen Jones, author of *To hell and back – Healing your way through transition*, says that guilt is a normal feeling for any mother: 'I don't know one mother who doesn't feel guilty about the times she thinks she has failed her child. The key is to be able to acknowledge the feeling for what it is and to learn from it. When you let go of the guilt, you can actually be a better, more relaxed mother.'

Of course, guilt is not all bad. To some degree, guilt is an essential emotion that maintains our moral fibre and keeps our conscience intact. Indeed, there are parents who would do well to feel more guilty about their inappropriate behaviour and parenting styles. Notwithstanding this, the guilt ingrained in most mothers is not a useful one. Whereas most emotions (including anger) mobilise us into action, guilt is immobilising. In previous generations, the culture of guilt was stronger as the mother played by the selfless rules of dedicating herself wholly to the children and the family. Unfortunately, guilt has continued to raise its ugly head as more women dedicate a large part of their lives to their careers.

Many mothers continue to carry the guilt, particularly through the turbulent years of adolescence. I no longer experience the same degree of guilt. I have found it easier with children now in their teens and beyond. But I do feel intermittent twinges. I feel guilty when I am repeatedly late for the pickup from school. I feel guilty when I haven't managed to get to the supermarket and we are out of milk or bread. I feel anxious and guilty when I leave for the airport on my frequent travels. But once aboard the aircraft, I let it go. It takes self-reflection and some effort, but it's possible and it's liberating.

WHAT TO DO:

- Don't feel alone – guilt is an inherent part of being a mother (but unusual for fathers!).
- Remember that other people cannot make you feel guilty about your mothering without your permission. They can try, but don't give them the power.
- Be aware that sometimes guilt can be helpful – for example, being able to apologise to your child when you are indeed wrong. But then let it go.
- Let go of perfectionism. As difficult as it is to change and shift from this, being a perfectionist is going to get in the way of effective mothering time and again.

32. SURRENDER

Q: How do I just surrender?

PARENT 1: I don't think he will manage this week at sleepover camp. I think I should phone the teacher and see if everything is okay.

PARENT 2: If I had been there, I could have prevented his car accident.

Having children is a lifelong lesson in feeling out of control. The fantasy that we are in control of their safety, wellbeing and life path is an illusion. You wield enormous influence over the development of his character, his personality, his sense of self and his education. But if we are totally honest, from the moment we give birth to a child, we surrender to forces that are greater than us. 'Surrender' is not a popular word in the 'I can do it all' generation. We imagine that to surrender is to lose or to experience defeat. We believe that every problem has a solution and every obstacle can be overcome. If anything goes wrong, then we try to fix it and if we can't, surely someone can. So much of the pain and heartache of parents everywhere, especially as their children develop into independent adolescents, derives from the sense that we have lost control over our children.

Jon Kabat Zinn, one of the pioneers of mindfulness, meditation and mind-body medicine, describes it all when he uses the term 'full catastrophe living' as the title of his seminal work. He uses the term not necessarily to describe disaster or tragedy, but rather 'the poignant enormity of our life experience'. When our child develops from an obedient, sweet youngster into a challenging adolescent and experiences the whole range of 'full catastrophe living', some of us adopt a punitive approach in the face of this challenge; others become permissive and just abandon their duty. The response to this phase in our child's life should not be to reject or dismiss him. Neither is it time, though, to throw up our hands in despair and relinquish responsibility. It is time to surrender. This means surrendering all our preconceived ideas and expectations. It means letting go of the old way of doing it. It is about moving from a micro-management leadership role (which is appropriate for toddlers and young children) into a macro-management role – no longer hovering like a helicopter over him but stepping back, surrendering and allowing him to move ably into his own space, just as you did when you let go of his hand so he could take his first steps alone. The answer I often get is, 'Ah! But I am not sure he can.'

Let go and see...

WHAT TO DO:

- Move from the micro-management style of parenting in the toddler and younger child years to a phase of macro-management for a more mature child.
- Don't let go of important boundaries but do let go of your sense of control.
- If you need to step back in again and hold on for a few more steps, then do so.
- Ideally, prepare for the letting go and surrendering long before he hits his teens.

33. DON'T BLAME AND SHAME

Q: Why do we end up blaming our teens unnecessarily?

MOTHER: That boy who fell on top of you caused the fracture!

SON: You've got it so wrong, Mum! It wasn't his fault at all. It was actually my fault. I tackled him.

MOTHER: What do you mean?

SON: We both tripped and he fell on top of me. It was an accident. And he was amazing, he picked me up and he was the only one to come with me to the office to find help. He was really kind.

. . . .

I am guilty. Today as I write these words, I am guilty of exactly what I am advising you not to do. Blaming my son or, even worse, someone else for something beyond his control. As I was sitting calmly writing the section on 'Surrender', knowing I had a welcome stretch of an afternoon ahead to continue writing undisturbed, I was rudely interrupted from my reverie.

The school number. My heart sinks. Ned has taken a bad fall playing soccer during break. He is in a lot of pain. Please get here soon. Just one glance at his tears and clenched jaw, and I know that it is certainly broken. He had tackled the biggest guy in his class, and I begin the blame game.

'Why did he fall on top of you? He is so much bigger than you. How did you let that happen? Why did you tackle him?'

I catch myself doing exactly what I promise myself I won't do. When I received an almost identical call a year earlier concerning my older son, Alex, I thought I had nothing to worry about. Twelve months, two teenage boys and three forearm fractures later, I am somewhat wiser. Alex's first two broken bones elicited enormous compassion and patience from me. By the third, I had lost my cool and lashed out at him for volunteering to play in a team of much older and bigger boys.

But more importantly, today unfolded into an even greater life lesson. We are under the illusion that we are here to teach and guide our children, whereas so much of the time we would do well to truly learn from them. In the middle of asking the whys and wherefores, I caught my breath and apologised. After all, my son had chosen not to apportion blame, but rather to take responsibility for his small part in the accident, and then to surrender to the reality of events outside of his control.

WHAT TO DO:

- We can avoid blaming and shaming our children for things that they are not responsible for. Know when to pick them out and when to show support and compassion.
- Be aware that much of what frustrates and inconveniences us or pushes our patience is not their fault.
- There are many circumstances when it is legitimate for our children to take the blame. If they have behaved badly, acted inappropriately, broken the law, the school rules or the family rules, they need to be reprimanded and feelings of guilt may in fact be appropriate in those circumstances.

34. SPOILT CHILD

Q: Am I spoiling my child?

DAD: But you've got a perfectly good cellphone.

SON: There is not one boy in my class who doesn't have an iPhone. I really need an iPhone.

DAD: But you don't need one. You've also got a computer and a camera and a Wii and a PlayStation.

SON: I so do! It's so cool. I need all the apps and all the cool things, and I can't possibly be the only one who doesn't have one.

Being spoilt is very closely related to the sense of entitlement so rife in this generation of teens (see 'Narcissism and entitlement' on page 86). However, in this section I am referring specifically to the ongoing acquisition of material things. A spoilt teen is one who gets too much stuff far too easily and whose world consists of acquiring more and more stuff because it's cool, because he wants it and because everyone else has it. All the 'cool stuff', particularly in this electronic generation, exerts an extremely strong pull on teens.

Kids have always liked nice clothes and cool things, and may have felt left out if they were deprived of them, but we seem to have taken consumerism to an obscene level. When it comes to children in general, and teens in particular, less is often more. There is considerable value in children having to learn to wait, to delay gratification, and often not getting what they want materially. The sooner they learn that in life you often don't get what you want, you have to work hard to achieve and acquire it, the better. They also learn immense gratitude when they get something that has required effort, or waiting or yearning. We do our children a major disservice by showering them with material things, particularly in response to their requests. They also need to be constantly reminded of those less fortunate than them.

- Even if you can afford it, resist acquiring an excessive amount of stuff for your teens.
- Don't allow your kids to pressure you, whether you can afford it or not.
- It's a good idea to encourage your teenager to get a part-time job and to use their earnings for all the 'cool stuff' they want. This is the best way to teach a teen the value of money. It is amazing how cautious he will become when having to spend his own money.

35. NARCISSISM AND ENTITLEMENT

Q: Why are our teens so self-entitled? Have we created a 'me monster'?

SON: I don't think that was my best soccer game. I didn't manage to play so well.

MUM: What are you talking about? You were superb, as always! You are the champion in that team.

SON: No, I could feel that I was missing lots of chances. It's no big deal. I'm fine about it.

MUM: No, you are an absolute superstar. By far the best player.

What has happened in the last 20 years that has led us to a state of such an overinflated and inappropriate sense of entitlement, particularly among our children? According to Dr Jean Twenge, professor of psychology at San Diego State University in the US, 'an extremely inflated view of self, and an overblown sense of entitlement' nowadays seem to define a whole generation of so-called normal individuals rather than a medical or psychiatric state, to which it refers. We are now more obsessed with ourselves and our children than ever. We cultivate and hero-worship the celebrity culture that screams 'look at me, me, me!'.

With society's extreme materialism and overconfidence about our children's abilities, are we as parents responsible for the creation of this 'me monster'? Some will argue that this generational spike in narcissism is due to social networking, particularly Facebook. Shawn Bergman, a professor of organisational psychology in North Carolina, believes that it has more to do with parents than online networking: 'Parents have overprotected their children more over the generations and have taught them to expect special treatment just for being them. This, in combination with the "self-esteem" movement, has likely resulted in increased narcissistic tendencies in our kids.' A great deal of research has substantiated Bergman's suggestion that obsessive parenting is possibly the biggest contributing cause.

Twenge reveals in her book *The epidemic of narcissism* that self-esteem itself does not breed success. Parents repeatedly informing kids how good they are, doling out undeserved praise, instils very little value and in fact may set up a false self. Children certainly thrive on love, and need to feel supported through life's challenges, but telling them they are the best in the world is not true and has very little value in building their character.

Although building self-esteem and confidence is important, we have gone overboard. The research demonstrates that extreme over-confidence often leads to disaster, both on a personal level and for society as a whole. On top of that, today's children are growing up in a culture that places heavy emphasis on being exceptional. Everyone wants to be exceptional. This outrageous epidemic is cultured in the Petri dish of infancy by parents who are dosing their children with a cocktail of obscene materialism and the message that they are more special than anybody else.

WHAT TO DO:

- Avoid lavishing praise for every small gesture. Ensure your praise is appropriate.
- Instead of trying to solve and eliminate your teens' struggles, allow them to figure things out, take criticism when necessary and accept the consequences of poor decisions.
- Back off and give your teen some space to express himself. Show love and concern, but there is no need to overinflate their sense of self.

36. FACE TIME

Q: How do I encourage my teenager to engage in some face-to-face time?

MUM: Come for dinner.

SON: I can't, I'm busy.

MUM: What are you busy with?

SON: Some stuff. I'll eat something later.

What we gain through face-to-face interaction is profound and cannot be replaced by any other form of communication. Reading each other's expressions, we gain valuable clues about how others are feeling. We learn to understand non-verbal cues, like body language, which express meaning. We share humour. We sense whether a person seems to be trusting, open and honest, or reserved and cautious. We also develop a mutual respect for one another. We gain all this through communicating face to face.

Our teens have been born into a world where this 'face time' experience is fading. Teens mainly connect with each other rapidly and frequently via texting and instant messaging. Being online with numerous people is stimulating, fun and easy for them. For many young teens who are immature and possibly awkward, chatting like this can be more comfortable than sitting face to face, talking to each other. Dr Daniel Goleman, psychologist, author and an expert on emotional intelligence, emphasises that social development occurs in the physical presence of other people and our brains process interactions among one another. If teens spend most of their social time behind a screen or a smartphone, they can become emotionally stunted without enough face time to learn the subtle yet vital aspects of empathy, caring and interactive skills. With face time they also learn to integrate and truly listen to another person in a way that just cannot occur in a text message. The high-speed nature of internet technology means teenagers often become extremely intolerant of the slower pace of time spent in the presence of 'real' people.

In business, politics and sport, successful leaders understand the importance of face-to-face contact. Duke University's coach, Mike Krzyzewski, the all-time most successful coach in American college basketball, told CNBC.com that face time is vital for unifying any group.

WHAT TO DO:

- Encourage periods of family face time with your children. Getting together for dinner is a great opportunity for face-to-face contact. If everyone is busy with extracurricular activities, try at least to set aside time once or twice a week for a family meal.
- It is commonplace nowadays for families and friends to sit together with everyone texting and no one paying attention to anyone else. Be firm that when you are together you should not all be focused on your phones. Encourage your teens to look at each other or you rather than at their phones.
- Turn off the television at dinner time.

37. HELICOPTER PARENTING ....

Q: I'm just very concerned for my child's welfare. Does this make me a helicopter parent?

TEACHER: Your child hasn't completed this project on time and will have to forfeit these marks.

MUM: I will ensure that she gets it done tonight.

TEACHER: No, I am afraid it's too late. She must learn the consequences of handing in work late.

MUM: She will have it on your desk first thing tomorrow.

TEACHER: You need to back off and allow your child to learn.

. . . .

The role of a helicopter is to hover, rescue and protect, and they play a vital role in emergency-response teams. But there is no need for them to hover and circle continuously when there is no emergency. Parents who insist on hovering, staying close by to provide constant protection, and then swooping in to 'rescue' their child from every issue, are termed 'helicopter parents'. You will have seen them hovering in and out of school, carrying extra bags, documents, assignments. They are sure to sit on every committee and are at school as often as the teachers. They are ready to swoop in, shield and rescue their offspring from any eventuality – demanding teachers, other kids or difficult assignments. 'Unfortunately they also shield their children from significant learning opportunities,' laments Foster Cline MD, author of *Parenting teens with love and logic.* Helicopter parents won't allow their kids to fail. They equate their child's mistakes or failings with poor parenting or a lack of concern on their part.

Cline draws attention to the fact that helicopter parents no longer just rescue their kids, they are obsessed with the desire to create a perfect life for their children, one in which they never have to face discomfort, struggle or disappointments. They drill them into awards, special honours and outstanding grades if possible, never stepping out of the way to allow their child to assume responsibility. 'These kids will often crash,' explains Cline, simply because their 'learning opportunities were stolen from them in the name of love.'

WHAT TO DO:

- Take a breath and try to observe your parenting style. If you fit this category, maybe it's time to take a step back.
- Although it's a tough world out there, hovering and overinvolvement do not provide an advantage for your teens. It robs them of their autonomy and diminishes their character and life-skill development.
- Raising competent, capable kids means backing off a bit to prepare them for the outside world.

38. TIGER PARENTING

Q: Is there value in tiger parenting?

SON: Kyle always gets the top marks for every test.

MOTHER: Well, that's good.

SON: He only gets those results because his parents push him so much.

MOTHER: Oh, that's interesting.

SON: Why don't you push me?

MOTHER: Well, most kids hate to be pushed! I thought you would appreciate a mother who doesn't push.

I got thinking about my parenting style after presenting a talk recently to the parents at one of Hong Kong's elite international schools, the emphasis there being on the pursuit of excellence and exceptional performance. I had always assumed that my own children would appreciate my lack of pushiness. A core parenting principle of mine is to enable my teenage kids to develop their own internal locus of control and responsibility for their work, even if it means lower grades in the short term. So it came as a surprise when my son Ned enquired in all seriousness why I don't push him in his education. I have found the rousing emotional responses to the book *Battle hymn of the tiger mother*, an analysis of Chinese parenting, most fascinating. Author Amy Chua, law professor at Yale University and mother of two teenage girls, sparked furious debate in the global media following the release of her book.

The debate began about Chinese mothering – Chua calls them 'tiger mums' – but has broadened beyond the Chinese to also include other Asian immigrants in North America, and the pressure on them to succeed: 'A lot of people wonder how Chinese parents raise such stereotypically successful kids – so many maths whizzes and prodigies. Well I can tell them, because I have done it,' explains Chua. She goes on to describe how her two daughters were never allowed to attend a sleepover, watch TV or play computer games. They were only permitted to play the violin and piano, and were not allowed to drop below an A grade at school. She says that even when Western parents think they are being strict, they don't come close to Chinese mothers. Chinese parents also do not allow kids to quit – which may be one kernel of wisdom we need to absorb from this parenting method. Many parents felt quite angry about Chua's approach. The Canadian *Globe & Mail* commented that Chua is 'probably the most reviled mother in the US'. But Judith Warner from the *New York Times* wrote: 'There was bound to be some push back…after all the years of overprotecting and obsessing with our children's self-esteem.'

This tiger approach has possibly given rise to a generation of self-entitled narcissists (see 'Narcissism and entitlement' on page 86). In the context of today's lack of boundaries, Amy Chua's philosophy has some value, but perhaps she has gone overboard.

We can perhaps take a word of wisdom from Hanna Rosin, editor of *The Atlantic* magazine, when she states that 'what privileged Western children need, is not more rules and maths drills. They need to express themselves and expand, not in ways dictated by their uptight overinvested parents.'

WHAT TO DO:

- Take a step back and truly observe your parenting style. If you are overinvesting for the sake of breeding success at all costs, perhaps begin to back off.
- Establish boundaries and basic expectations for behaviour and performance, but ensure that you are realistic and compassionate in setting them out.
- What we can learn from tiger parents is not to allow our kids to quit too easily when things get tough.

39. DO WE F*** THEM UP?

Q: Do we as parents screw up our kids?

They fuck you up, your mum and dad.

They may not mean to, but they do.

They fill you with the faults they had

And add some extra, just for you.

'This be the verse' – PHILIP LARKIN

The famous English poet Philip Larkin held an extremely pessimistic view on parenting.

Do we really f*** them up? Sure, there are some awful parents out there. But the vast majority of parents have the best intentions. We certainly don't want to be messing them up. We want to raise well-mannered, hard-working, morally upright individuals. We want happy children, healthy children and, let's be honest, we all want them to succeed in their endeavours. But often our own personal upbringing, our misguided aspirations for our children or our reluctance to see our children objectively can get in the way.

In *How not to f*** them up*, author and unconventional British child psychologist Oliver James argues that it's not our children who must be trained, it's us.

Debates over how to parent are as old as parenting itself and there are as many different psychological theories and approaches as there are families. Parents (especially mothers) know they will be blamed if their kids don't turn out right. And so we worry. Although we seem to be confronted constantly by the media and a barrage of research showing how easy it is to screw up your kids, Donald Winnicott's ground-breaking work and world view hold strong. This influential English paediatrician and child psychiatrist argued that you don't have to be a perfect mother to raise a well-adjusted kid. You just have to be, to use the term Winnicott coined, a 'good-enough mother'.

Let's hear what the experts have to say on how to avoid the fundamental f***-up areas:

WHAT TO DO:

- Don't lie to your child, urges Dr L. Alan Sroufe, professor emeritus of psychology at the University of Minnesota's Institute of Child Development.
- Don't ignore your own bad behaviour, implores child development expert Dr David Elkind, professor emeritus of child development at Tufts University and well-known child development author.
- Don't try to be your child's friend rather than his parent. This is a common mistake that parents make, particularly as their kids get older, warns Dr Sue Hubbard, paediatrician and US parenting author.
- Don't overindulge your teen. 'Overindulgence is probably the easiest way to mess up your kid,' contends Dr Twenge.

40. COMMON INTERESTS: 'MUM, HAVE YOU HEARD OF BOB DYLAN?'

Q: How can we find areas of common interest with our teens?

SON: Mum! Quick! Come downstairs and listen to this.

MOTHER: What is it?

SON: I think you will really like this. Listen to this song I just downloaded.

MOTHER: Okay, coming down.

SON: Mum, have you ever heard of Bob Dylan? I love this stuff.

MOTHER: Of course I have! I was listening to Bob Dylan long before you were born.

Teenage years are notorious for tantrums, conflict and misery, but there can also be something thrilling about watching a child develop his own passions, and sometimes you even discover common interests.

A few weeks ago, my youngest son, Ned, aged 13, asked excitedly if I had heard of Bob Dylan. Oh my goodness! The brief trip down a flight of stairs to his room became a profound journey back in time. 'How many roads must a man walk down...' The flood of memories engulfed me: camp fires, old boyfriends, university protests, hikes through the mountains with those words reverberating through my head. In the past year, Ned has become increasingly interested in and passionate about retro music. The interest was sparked by the Beatles, moved on to Pink Floyd and the Rolling Stones, and now encompasses all music from the 50s to the 80s. He spends hours collecting and listening to music, reading the history of these eras, and has even persuaded his piano and saxophone teachers to switch from the classics at times and teach him to play Beatles compositions. Although his brain 'explosion' (as described in 'A new life stage' on page 15) has certainly produced some of the adolescent traits, such as challenging authority, it has also led to a new, exciting passion.

It is refreshing as a parent to watch a child's passion grow. It is also rewarding when our child is able to guide or inspire us in a field of interest and thereby build common ground. It is encouraging for the teenager too, when his parents are genuinely interested. I think as parents we can possibly celebrate a lot more and shout a little less through this time.

My son is still not convinced that I really do know who Bob Dylan is. And when the song is over, he asks if I can please leave his room and close the door. But that's okay. To be honest with you, if I think back to his toddler years ('Pleeease stay in my room and do one more puzzle'), I don't mind being shut out and getting back to what I was doing before he discovered Bob Dylan.

WHAT TO DO:

- Take an interest in what your teenager is doing. Try to discover areas where you may have a common interest and nurture them.
- If your children are keen to spend some time with you, seize the moment.
- It's common for dads and sons to go to sports games, but try to support other interests, such as photography exhibitions or science fairs.
- Aim to have fun together by doing what they are keen to do, such as shopping or practising driving.
- Spend some time listening to their music.
- Communicate via email: send them articles or things that may interest them.

41. OWN THE PROBLEM . . . .

Q: Is this behaviour due to him keeping bad company?

FATHER: You can't lie to me anymore. I got a call from your teacher today. They caught you guys smoking at school again.

SON: It wasn't really me.

FATHER: What do you mean?

SON: Well, I was just hanging out with the guys behind the canteen while they were smoking.

FATHER: The smoking is bad enough let alone your lying.

. . . .

When things don't go according to our expectations it is easy to find an extraneous reason. We are called in by the school for our child's unacceptable behaviour, or discover that he has been binge drinking or experimenting with marijuana. The first major mistake we make is to blame someone else. We blame the child's friends, we blame the school, we blame the internet – anything but accept that our child is wholly responsible for his misdeeds. It may feel uncomfortable to accept that our child has behaved badly, but it is wise to look inward, not outward, in response to this type of situation, explains Dr Sue Hubbard, paediatrician and US parenting author.

First, identify the problem. Accept there is a problem and help your child own up to the misdemeanour. The child needs to know from the outset that the first step is to take responsibility and 'own' the problem. Even if other children are involved, that's not your family's concern. There is nothing to be gained by diminishing your child's involvement. The sooner you are able to accept that your child has crossed a line, the quicker your child will be able to accept responsibility. The next step is to make your teenager aware that there are consequences for all behaviours – good and bad. If other people were hurt in the process, apologies are imperative. Then the consequences, such removing privileges, should be implemented. This depends on the age of your child and your family's rules system. But be sure to impose some form of punitive follow-up.

Making light of the situation, minimising the problem and blaming others are all strategies that contribute to the proverbial f***ing up (see page 94). It is extremely difficult for parents to admit they have a child who has stepped out of line. Unfortunately, parents can't help feeling that it reflects badly on them. I believe it is essential to separate our emotions from the situation and do the right thing. If you are in the midst of a crisis, do not ignore the problem and hope it will go away. It won't. The problem will fester until it becomes much more inflamed. Lance the ugly wound now and allow healing and improvement to take place.

WHAT TO DO:

- Help your child take responsibility for the problem. Don't blame friends. If your teen is involved, he is just as responsible as the other members of the group.
- Do not ignore a problem and hope it will disappear. It never does. It usually gets worse.
- Face up to it and intervene with courage as well as compassion.
- Do not expend too much energy getting them to say 'I did it'. Instead express your strongest disapproval as well as the consequences, and move away.
- You may require professional advice.

42. DAUGHTERS: A MOTHER'S MIRROR

Q: How do I pass on good values to my daughter?

DAUGHTER 1: You are exactly like Mum.

DAUGHTER 2: OMG! No ways! You've got to be joking!

For some strange reason, being told you are exactly like your mum is never really a compliment. When you are the mother, however, you cannot understand why your daughter would not want to be just like you.

A few weeks ago, I found myself in an argument with both my twin daughters at the same time. I had made a casual remark that I had heard from a fellow mother about the behaviour of some kids from the same class as our son at a school-prom party. I was seriously unimpressed by the behaviour and expressed my sense of shock to my own children. My daughters both became quite angry with me that I had listened to gossip. They also disagreed with my moral view. Eventually Leigh withdrew from the discussion, leaving Elle and me bickering away. The emotions flared and neither of us would back down. It ended with her in tears. She was upset by my tone and forcefulness, and felt I had been nasty. I couldn't understand this, as I thought she was the one raising her voice. I overheard Leigh whisper to her brother, who nodded in agreement, 'OMG, Mum and Elle are identical! They were both shouting at each other, both getting emotional, both not giving up.' I had not seen myself through this interaction. I only saw Elle's emotional irrationality, but this was clearly the way I was behaving too. Though I apologised and we made up later that evening, I realised with shock that I, the mother, was behaving just like the kid embroiled in an adolescent power struggle.

As mothers, how we respond to our daughters is shaped by our unique personal experiences, which include our childhood, religious and cultural perspectives, and our world view. Whatever we do, we cannot control how our daughters will respond to our mothering. Mothers have always been glorified and have also always been blamed. The relationship between a mother and a daughter has the potential for real emotional closeness as well as disappointment and anger. Pennsylvania State University researcher Professor Karen Fingerman's study on the ties between adult daughters and their elderly mothers found that despite conflicts and complicated emotions, the mother-daughter bond is so strong that 80 per cent of women at midlife report good relationships with their mothers.

Our daughters learn much more from what we do than what we say. They watch us and learn how to be a woman. They learn about being happy or unhappy, about being married or divorced, about embracing life or complaining frequently, about food and sex and alcohol, in ways we cannot imagine. They look into our mirror and absorb or reject many aspects of who we are. They watch us in ways we cannot control. We can only behave and model integrity and love and compassion. The only way to pass on qualities is to live them.

WHAT TO DO:

- We may be mirrors for our daughter but sometimes we see ourselves reflected in them.
- We may sometimes need to apologise for our mistakes and our behaviours.
- It's a great learning opportunity for our children to witness our weaknesses and shortcomings, especially if we are able to apologise.
- Pass on to your teens your most valued qualities by living them.

43. MOTHERS' MISTAKES

Q: What mothering mistakes do you think your daughters would like to avoid?

MOTHER: What aspects of your mother's behaviour would you choose to emulate or reject?

CAITLIN: I would never want to be as overinvolved as she is in my life. I'd give more space.

SARAH: I would be more available for my kids. Mum's too busy all the time.

SAMMY: I would be much less strict.

. . . .

At a recent focus group with high-school girls, I conducted a brief survey asking them how they would do things differently if they one day became mothers. I asked what mistakes they would try to avoid and what aspects of their mothers' behaviour they would emulate or reject.

The answers were as varied as the girls. Some complained of mothers who were too busy for them, whereas others said quite the opposite – their mothers were overinvolved and too focused on them. There are girls who complain their mums are distant, while others feel smothered. Some feel that their mums don't tell them anything; others feel uncomfortable that their mothers share too much information. It's hard for a mother to know exactly what to do. It is true that an extreme approach in either direction is not good, but it is not always easy to find the middle ground.

I asked my own daughters what they would do differently and what mistakes I had made:

DAUGHTER 1: I wouldn't go away while my children were writing exams (ouch!).

DAUGHTER 2: I would never be late to fetch them from school or a lesson (ouch! ouch!).

DAUGHTER 1: I would send my daughters to ballet. Truly, Mum, what kind of mother doesn't send her cute twin girls to ballet? (A sporty mum who could never dance.)

DAUGHTER 2: I would push them much more. You let me give up swimming lessons before I even got the strokes right and now I am a poor swimmer.

Okay, anything else? Enough love? *Yeah!* Enough communication? *Yeah!* Enough encouragement but not too pushy? *Yeah, sure.* Enough space to express yourself? *Yip.* Enough empathy? *Yes, Mum, enough talking!*

I have tried to improve my punctuality. I am aiming not to be away during exams again. As for the ballet, swimming and being away during stressful times, they will have to take those issues to the therapist's couch. It could always be much worse.

WHAT TO DO:

- The important thing is to be loving, compassionate and empathetic; you cannot be what you are not.
- Be honest and keep the channels of communication open.
- Be true to yourself and your values.
- As Dr Winnicott put it, 'be a good-enough mother'.
- You will make mistakes. That's okay – you are human. Apologise and move on.

44. FAT PHOBIA

Q: How can we try not to pass on our own distorted body issues?

DAUGHTER: Mum, you are very lucky that none of your children have developed eating disorders.

MOTHER: (Stunned silence)

Recently at dinner, while complaining that regardless of how I have cut down my calories and increased my exercise, I just cannot rid myself of this stubborn muffin-top midriff, I received a surprising comment from Leigh: 'Mum, you are very lucky that none of your children have developed eating disorders!'

I was stunned. I had no words, but powerful thoughts flew through my head. 'What are you talking about? I have brought you all up with a healthy eating consciousness. I have almost never used the word "diet". What do you mean?...'

Without me giving a response, she continued: 'You are so obsessed with being overweight. Even though you think you are fat and say you have put on four kilos over the past few years, you don't look fat. And even if you did, Dad doesn't mind. Why don't you believe us? You look fine. I mean really, you are 48! Who do you want to be thin for? Why do you want to be thin?'

Instead of bursting into tears, I chuckled quietly to myself. 'You are 48! Why do you want to be thin?' I may be the mother and the doctor and the health expert, but I am also a woman who still wants to feel and look good. I also bring to my parenting my own childhood and family issues. I come from a family that is overweight. My grandfather was fairly round and my mother and sister have had a fluctuating significant weight problem for as long as I can remember. I therefore have a fat phobia. I am petrified of being fat. I have to watch myself very carefully and when I gain weight and see myself in the mirror, I see an obese woman. I know I am not truly obese – but the image is distorted by my fear. I am fully conscious and aware of this issue. And I have been cautious not to hand it down to my children. Luckily for them, I feel, in the main they have inherited their dad's family genes of a long, lean body. I have been conscious throughout their upbringing to focus on the health aspects related to food – the brain power, the energy fuel of nutritious power food – rather than the dieting approach. Journalist and author Linda Valdez says: 'We tell our daughters that they can do what they want. We send these messages while we run to lose weight. We talk about being independent and powerful, but we obsess about being fat.'

WHAT TO DO:

- Be honest about your own issues about food and express these issues openly.
- Try to be clear about the verbal and non-verbal messages you give your daughter. She watches you more than she hears.
- Be aware and conscious of your own incongruous behaviours and be able to listen to her criticism too.

45. PARENTING BOYS

Q: What are the secrets to raising great male teens?

DAD: What's happening? What are you doing this evening?

SON: Nothing much, Dad. Just hanging out.

DAD: Let's go for a bike ride?

SON: Great!

. . . .

'To become a good man, you have to know good men,' emphasises Stephen Biddulph, an eminent child psychologist who has sold more than four million copies of *Raising boys*. 'Fathers,' he says, 'are boys' security and role models.' He explains how a decade ago, boys were five times more likely to have problems in school and three times more likely to die before the age of 21. This is no longer the case, Biddulph believes, because parenting has improved vastly and the main change is that fathers are playing their part.

Although Biddulph does not advocate different approaches to bringing up the two sexes, there are distinctions worth noting between the genders. He frequently emphasises the significance of a strong father figure or male role model for boys. He describes that although mothers are important for a boy's self-esteem, it is fathers that can turn boys into men who are communicative and sensible. He also emphasises that male mentors, such as teachers and sports coaches, are important to 'initiate' boys into manhood. Biddulph highlights the importance of a boy 'leaving' his mother and becoming a man.

Biddulph gives the following best tips for raising boys into great men:

- Give children understanding and time, he advises parents, not criticism and money. 'You may be busy at work, but every event you share with a child – whether the game you play when stuck in traffic, or the kite you fly together – is like a diamond on a necklace.'
- Fathers should not be afraid to show emotion to their sons and should encourage their sons to express their own emotions.

- Help boys develop a healthy sexuality by encouraging open communication and positive messages about dignity and love.
- Boys should be socialised with girls so that they develop a healthy sense of what females are like.

FRIENDS AND RELATIONSHIPS

FRIENDS AND THE PEER GROUP are extremely important to adolescents. 'The teen defers to the power and influence of the group,' explains Serenne Kaplan, South African psychotherapist and adolescent expert. 'Their need to fit in and attain approval and acceptance is at its height at this stage.'

For obvious reasons, parents are concerned about the type of company their teen keeps, the quality of the friends and the influence of the peer group. The peer group has significant value in the development of an adolescent and can have positive influences. However, combating the negative influence of peer pressure begins long before your child reaches adolescence. A common parental error is that when we sense bad behaviour in our children, we assume it is the bad influence of another child. Parents are often reluctant to accept that the misconduct is not necessarily the influence of the friend but may reflect their own child's behaviour.

This chapter explores how, although as parents it is important to maintain a strong sense of surveillance, we should avoid hovering too closely and misjudging. Often our teens will discover for themselves which friendships work and which don't. As parents, we are fiercely protective of our offspring. We worry if they are too shy or lack self-confidence; we want our children to be social; we want them to have friends and enjoy happy teen years. But some kids are naturally introverts and may be at peace with that. We also want to protect them from being hurt, particularly when falling in love. Don't make the mistake of minimising teen love and heartaches, which can be very real and intense. This chapter also provides some insight into the significant shift taking place in adolescence – when the child moves away from the parent as the main source of strong attachment and extends strong feelings of attachment to others.

46. BAD INFLUENCE

Q: My child's friend is a really bad influence. What should I do?

DAD: You are impossible when you've been with Jake!

SON: What are you talking about?

DAD: Have you been drinking now at his house?

SON: Don't be stupid!

DAD: You see, you are so rude after you have been with him! Who knows what else you two get up to. I don't want you to spend time with him.

SON: I can't believe this!

. . . .

We are fiercely protective of our offspring. As soon as we sense a bad influence on our child, we want to do something immediately to stop it. Being hasty is not a good idea though. Before attempting to banish the bad influence, we need to take a step back and review the situation. Parents are often reluctant to accept that the misconduct or sloppy behaviour is not necessarily the influence of the friend but may be inherent in their own child's behaviour (see also 'Own the problem' on page 98). It may even be possible that the other parent feels that their son is badly influenced by yours. Adopt a vigilant approach and observe what's going on. We need to establish some sound evidence before attributing bad behaviours to the friend or the crowd.

WHAT TO DO:

- Be clear with your son that you are concerned about his behaviour and be specific about what behaviours are bothering you, rather than criticising generalised behaviour. For example: 'You have come home late on four separate occasions despite warnings', or 'You are extremely rude in his company'.
- Even though certain behaviours may have begun when this friend arrived on the scene, focus on your son's need to buck up.
- Avoid accusing his friend. This is a time to keep your mouth shut

for the moment. If you attack, he is most likely to defend his friend and possibly become secretive.

- Monitoring and surveillance are appropriate in this case. Be vigilant and aware of anything untoward.
- If you discover any illegal activity or breaking of the family rules, you could then enforce a break in socialising with this particular friend (or crowd) for a set period of time.
- Stay calm, as these are situations where you will experience emotional dumping of anger and frustration.

47. SHYNESS

Q: What can I do to help my painfully shy daughter socialise better?

DAUGHTER: I'm not going!

MUM: You can't miss another friend's party.

DAUGHTER: You can't force me, now leave me alone!

MUM: You have to make an effort or you won't have any friends.

DAUGHTER: I am happy with Sophie. I don't need any more friends.

MUM: Just try to make an effort. Get out there, dance a bit, have fun.

DAUGHTER: I hate those parties! I don't want to go. Leave me alone.

One of the great challenges of parenting is to accept our teens' inborn temperaments and manage their issues in a constructive way, and in a way that is best for them. They are not clones of their parents. It is often very difficult for an extrovert to parent a shy child. They just don't understand what goes on in the head or heart of a shy teen, in much the same way that an introverted parent may struggle with an exuberant teenager.

There is often a great deal of concern about a shy teenager. We worry about their lack of self-esteem if they don't have lots of friends, and whether our shy child will develop the necessary life skills. We want our children to be social people. We want them to have friends and enjoy happy teenage years. Perhaps we shouldn't be too concerned, however. Although there is a connection between introversion and shyness, they are different entities. Introverts prefer solitary pursuits to social events but they are not necessarily anxious or fearful about socialising. What worries parents is the reluctance or refusal of the teen to initiate or participate in social activities. With painfully shy children, their refusal to be social is often based on genuine feelings of anxiety and fear, which may require some form of intervention.

- Avoid showing disdain or labelling the shyness. It gives the message 'we wish you were different'.
- Focus on building her strong points. If she loves animals or photography, encourage these things.
- Do not laud popularity and crowds of friends per se. There is no inherent value in them, particularly for a shy child.
- If she has one or two people she considers friends and doesn't complain of being lonely, then back off and let her be.
- If she attends a few social events, such as a school festival or family gathering, without huge resistance then her social skills are probably not something to cause concern.
- Being a spectator rather than a participant is perfectly normal. Not everyone chooses to be in the centre of activities.
- Some kids do not enjoy crowds or parties at all, and this is a normal and perfectly healthy way to grow up.
- If she demonstrates genuine dread, panic or significant anxiety about social interaction, it is valuable to engage the assistance of a therapist or counsellor.

48. PEER PRESSURE

Q: What should a parent do to counteract peer pressure?

DAD: Where are you going?

SON: To hang out at Todd's place.

DAD: What's happening there?

SON: The usual. Just hanging out. A few drinks, some friends, nothing major.

DAD: Take it easy. As we've talked about before, be aware of what you choose to do. You don't need to go overboard and binge drink because everyone else is doing that.

Although as parents we worry about the power peer pressure exerts on our teens, it's not all bad news. The peer group has significant value in the development of an adolescent and can indeed have positive influences. It is a normal aspect of a young person's development to want to fit into their social group and receive approval from their peers. This need for approval is a powerful trigger for many of their actions, conducts and behaviours, both good and bad.

We want to minimise the peer-group pressure to engage in risky, illegal and troublesome behaviours. Combating the negative influence of peer pressure, however, begins long before your child reaches adolescence. We hope that the lessons we've taught them will stay with them and that they will be strong enough to resist the temptation to veer from what they know is the right thing. But the truth is, this really depends on the age of the child. Researchers Laurence Steinberg and Kathryn Monahan from the University of Washington in the US suggest that 'children are most vulnerable to peer pressure between the ages of 10 and 14. After that, resistance to peer pressure increases linearly until the age of 18. After that, it seems to hold steady.'

According to another recent study by Joanna Chango, *Predictors of peer pressure*, 'teens who are able to express their own views with their mothers resist peer pressure the best. That is, the teens who have learned to argue well with their mothers were the best at standing up to peer influences.' Predictably, teenagers with the greatest sense of autonomy and self-confidence are the most resistant to peer pressure.

WHAT TO DO:

- Although the influence of peers is a normal part of a teen's development, they require help and support from parents to resist the pressures, especially negative influences.
- Be open and honest about it. Talk about the issue of peer pressure. Let them know that you believe that a lot of the influence is good but that some of it is problematic.
- Don't lecture. Allow your teen to express himself.
- Teach them how to say no and that it's okay to say no and still maintain their place in the crowd. Allow them to blame you for refusing to let them attend certain events or activities.
- Throughout their upbringing, encourage them to feel comfortable to hold views and opinions that are different from yours. This will help build the strengths required to hold views and indulge in behaviours that are different from the crowd.
- Respected Australian parenting professional Michael Grose suggests assisting kids with techniques to resist the pressure. One such simple peer-resistance strategy involves taking time to consider something: 'A comeback line such as, "No, not now. I'll think about it later" helps them buy some time and still maintain credibility among the group.'
- Encourage them to stop and think through the consequences before embarking on any risky behaviour.
- Attempt to outline the behaviours you dislike rather than criticising the friends. They take such criticism very personally and you will gain no ground.

49. TEENS IN LOVE

Q: Is it normal for my teen to be head over heels in love?

MUM: You'll get over it.

DAUGHTER: You just don't understand! How can I ever get over it?

MUM: This happens to everyone, darling. It's not such a big deal.

DAUGHTER: Leave me alone!

Don't make light of teen love and heartaches. These feelings are very real and often particularly intense. It is a mistake for parents to downplay and mock these genuine emotions. Contrary to popular belief, teens do experience emotions other than sexual feelings. Although surging sexual awareness is powerful in adolescence, so too are deep feelings of love. During adolescence there is a marked shift away from the parent as the main target of attachment and strong feelings of attachment become focused on others.

There is obviously a whole gamut of what adolescent love may entail, from an immature teenage crush right through to an older adolescent's mature relationship. 'Teen love is disconcerting to parents,' suggests Dr Anthony Wolf, author of *The secret of parenting*, 'because it often appears to be so strong and all consuming.' It is a powerful force, and seems to remove your influence over your child. However, falling in love is an important aspect of their development, and a process through which they begin to care deeply about someone other than themselves. Nevertheless, teens in love often land up miserable and overwrought. There are frequent split-ups and heartbreaks along the way. Although it is usually best not to interfere, if you find that a relationship is detrimental to your teen's life, it may be necessary to intervene. If school work is affected or your child is frequently miserable, your support and guidance are required. Be present for your child during break-ups, keep channels of communication open and provide a warm, supportive environment.

- Don't mock or belittle your teen's love interest: be aware that this is an important aspect of their development and the feelings are real.
- Try not to be judgemental and make yourself available should your teen want to talk.
- Communication channels are essential. You could use the relationship as a springboard for discussion, and issues around sexuality need to be discussed (see 'Sex and teens' on page 191).
- Stay involved with your child. Hopefully, the relationship will be successful but be aware that many teenage love relationships collapse. Your teen will need your non-judgemental love and support through this painful time.
- If there is a break-up, acknowledge what a painful process this is. Be there to give support and comfort, but don't pry.

50. IS MY CHILD GAY?

Q: How do I know if my son is gay?

MUM: I think you are wonderful and I love you and accept you regardless. Are you gay?

SON: Are you mad! You think I'm gay!?

MUM: I think you're fabulous and I wouldn't love you any less.

SON: I can't believe this! Gay! Are you crazy?

What is my child's sexual preference? This is a frequently asked question: 'How do I know if my son/daughter is gay? How can I find out or ask?' If you suspect that your child is gay, your suspicion may be correct, or you may be wrong. Many parents want to ask their teenager and get an honest, direct answer. But no matter how you pose the question, it may be hurtful and detrimental. The response given by the son ('Are you mad! You think I'm gay!?') would be appropriate if he weren't gay but it might also be the response if he were gay. He may not want to reveal his sexual preference to you. As with any adolescent guy, he would not want to share any details of sex or his sexuality with his parents.

Serenne Kaplan suggests it is best to allow your teen to share this information with you when and if he chooses to and not to ask this question. What you could do to make it easier for your child if you suspect he is gay is to display a positive attitude and understanding that being gay is not shameful. Attempt to demonstrate to your child that he is loved regardless of his sexual preference.

As one mother in a recent focus group suggests, 'for families struggling with this new information, one of the best ways to come to terms with the realisation and understanding of having a gay son or lesbian daughter is to gain as much information as possible. And keep asking questions so that you eventually understand their new lives.'

WHAT TO DO:

• Do not try to find out whether he is gay or not. He will share it with you when he is ready.

119

- Ensure your attitude towards being gay is accepting and tolerant.
- Try to make it known through your interactions and exchange of ideas with others that you are non-judgemental of a gay lifestyle.
- If you do have bigoted ideas about a gay lifestyle, it is worth re-thinking your attitudes and possibly even talking them through with a counsellor.
- You cannot change someone who is gay. That is the way it is. He doesn't really make a choice about it. All you can control or alter is your own attitude and mind-set.
- Your son/daughter needs consistent love and acceptance.

If your teen does tell you he is gay:
- Be as calm as possible.
- Be honest and explain that you may not understand, but you want to.
- Be patient and give him time. Don't expect to have every question answered in the first conversation.
- Don't make negative or confrontational comments, especially if you want to keep communication open.
- Find someone to talk to – but not just anyone. 'The parents in my study were helped by talking to a trusted friend, relative or co-worker or a professional therapist. These trustworthy confidants let them vent but also corrected some of the misperceptions they absorbed from society,' explains Dr Michael La Sala, associate professor at the State University of New Jersey and author of *Coming out, coming home: Helping families adjust to a gay or lesbian child*.
- Let your teen know that you love him or her unconditionally.
- Do praise your teen for sharing his or her feelings.

BEHAVIOURS

YOU HAVE SPENT THE LAST 12 years drilling your child about courteousness and decent behaviour. So what has happened? All of a sudden, you are faced with rudeness, belligerence and confrontation. This may be a sign of surging hormones and the emerging adolescent self trying to chop down the parents' authority to make place for his own. It is also explained by leading neuroscientists as the 'exploding teen brain', which causes decent behaviour to come undone. 'Self-absorbed, preoccupied and wound up in themselves, living in all-about-me bubbles is a totally normal thing for adolescents,' explains Dr Laura Kastner, clinical associate professor of behavioural sciences at the University of Washington in the US.

This chapter looks at some of the unpleasant behaviours you may experience – selfishness, defiance, disobedience, anger and rebelliousness – and provides the experts' advice on how best to guide your teen through this new stage and identity. Also be aware that many teens save the worst for home, where they can 'dump' after the restraining environment of school, with its rules and regulations.

Many teens, however, are able to retain a sense of morality, good character and well-mannered behaviour through the turbulence of adolescence. More often than not, such teenagers experience neither overtly controlling parenting nor smothering love but are given the space to develop themselves, disagree and challenge parental beliefs. The good news is that even defiant teens will grow out of their egocentricism and bad conduct, especially if parents play their cards right by avoiding power struggles, which make teens keep up their resistance to parents' controlling ways. By about 15 or 16, they usually begin to see things less myopically and have a broader perspective, and hence their behaviour shifts.

51. RUDENESS

Q: How should I respond to my terribly rude 13-year-old?

MUM: I brought you a snack to eat before the soccer game.

SON: I'm not hungry.

MUM: You need some energy.

SON: Are you deaf? I told you I'm not hungry.

Rudeness may sneak up on parents in a flash. It may just entail rolling his eyes to the ceiling or throwing dirty looks, or it may be as serious as showing blatant disrespect. As parents, it's hard not to take such rudeness personally. It is embarrassing, it is hurtful and it seems to reflect bad character, not only in the child but also the parents.

As awful as it is for parents, this dreadful conduct and disrespect are a sign of the emergence of a new life stage and a new identity in your child. Laura Kastner calls this the 'second autonomy phase'. The terrible twos, signalling the emergence of a defiant, independent toddler, is the first autonomy phase. During this second phase, the rejection of a parent's authority and value system feels intensely painful. But that is what this phase is all about: the emergent autonomous self is trying to chop down the parents' authority to make place for his own. He needs to build assertive and expressive skills. Unfortunately he is often off the mark and comes across as downright insolent. He requires guidance through this phase. We often say, 'I never spoke to my parents like this.' It is true. And the style of parenting has changed too. We are far less keen to use threats and fear and scare tactics, which are intimidating and dictatorial. This authoritarian approach will engender less rudeness but it can also backfire and cause rebellion. We certainly want some level of obedience but we should place great value on communication, connectedness and self-worth.

WHAT TO DO:

• Rudeness indicates a new developmental period, and for this we need new tools. It is easy to crack down hard, but it doesn't usually succeed – it fuels the power struggle. And permissiveness without authority is unproductive.

- Determine if this is all-pervasive rudeness or just happens at home. The rudeness often manifests only at home when children are frustrated, having a bad day and you're in the way.
- If they are rude with everyone, including teachers and authority figures, you may need some professional intervention.
- Ignore the rudeness much of the time. Don't give it power.
- Tackle it directly and without emotion. Rather than saying, 'Don't you dare talk to me that way!' just say, 'Cut it out.'
- Don't give in to what they want. The rudeness usually comes after you have said no to something. Stand your ground.

52. MANNERS

Q: How do you teach a teenager manners?

DAD: Hello, Steve.

DAD: Hello, Steve.

DAD: Steve!

SON: Can't you see, I'm on my cellphone!

You have spent at least 12 years drilling the 'pleases' and 'thank yous', respect for elders, making eye contact, behaving courteously. So what has happened to these manners? Teens know very well how to use them when something important is at stake. They are still there but have become submerged as pubertal hormones, mood swings and a new attitude emerge. They also save the worst for home, where they can dump, having restrained their impulses and followed rules all day at school. Once again, the 'teen brain' intervenes and all decent behaviour seems to come undone.

Although teens have an aversion to rules, this is not the time to give up on fostering manners. But choose carefully because your list of directives needs to be short. 'When it comes to teaching manners to teenagers, think feelings, not fussy rules,' explains Thomas Farley, manners expert, *New York Times* contributor and editor of *Modern manners: The thinking person's guide to social graces*. 'Manners, at their core, are being aware of how your actions are going to make other people feel. People with poor manners are more likely to hurt other people's feelings – and hurt feelings are something young people can relate to,' says Farley. Kids will tune out discussions about rules but you may be able to engage them in a conversation about feelings.

WHAT TO DO:

- Teach teenagers the importance of a proper greeting. It is important to look someone in the eye and say hello when being introduced. Sometimes a handshake is in order.
- Being kind is often one of the most forgotten forms of etiquette.

Teenagers are focused so intensely on themselves that they forget common decency. No matter what the situation, kindness is always appropriate. Stress the need to take other people's feelings into consideration with the things they do and say.

- It seems common sense, but allowing and listening to someone else's opinion are essential. Teenagers can be incredibly opinionated and their views can come across in a rude way. Teach your teenagers to share their opinions in a respectful manner.

- Cellphone etiquette has become an essential point of training in the corporate world. Teens have no clue that there is even such a thing, but we can begin to teach them. They should know that it is not acceptable to ignore someone who is trying to get their attention while they are on the phone – they need to pause their conversation and answer; it is rude to talk on a cellphone at the table with other people present; they should never shout into the phone; turn it onto silent or vibrate mode when somewhere quiet.

- There are countless opportunities for demonstrating good manners. Don't give up on this essential area of their development into a decent adult.

53. LYING

Q: How can I trust him again after he lied to us?

SON: Hi, Mum. Wow, I'm so tired! We didn't get much sleep at Tim's sleepover last night.

MUM: Hang on a moment. Don't make it worse than it already is. I just found out the truth.

SON: What are you talking about?

MUM: I know you guys drove four hours to the concert and slept in the park – after I said you couldn't go.

SON: How did you find out?

MUM: Just tell me the truth and tell me what happened.

Parents justifiably go into a headspin when they discover their child has lied to them. Honesty is one of the cornerstones of morality that we want our children to embody, and most parents react severely to lying. Nevertheless, most teenagers will occasionally tell a lie to their parents in order to get what they want or to get out of trouble. We all hope our children will never lie to us but a once-off untruth does not mean they cannot grow up to be honest adults, especially if they have honest parents who deal appropriately with their issues and emotions.

Every family has its specific rules that are sacred. In our family, honesty is one of those issues that stands supreme. My children have known since early childhood that telling lies is tantamount to stealing or cheating. But that is our family rule book. You will have your own, which may (or may not) be more lenient. If, however, you discover the lying is an ongoing problem and is part of a pattern of deceit and denial, this is a serious matter (beyond the scope of this book), and it requires professional intervention. Many families value honesty but some develop patterns that in reality hinder honesty. When parents themselves lie, it breeds a dysfunctional, messy family life and you cannot expect honesty from your children in that sort of environment. In such cases, counselling is strongly advised.

- Be direct and address the issue up front. Do not try to catch your child out to see whether he will cover up or reveal the truth.
- Be sure that you uphold a code of honesty before moralising. If you do not honour that value, you cannot expect your kids to respect it.
- Don't mince your words. Say it like it is: lying is a terrible thing. You need to determine where the deceit is coming from and turn it around so it doesn't happen again.
- Although we need to communicate the moral issues about how lying destroys trust between people and how important it is to maintain a strong code of honesty, also acknowledge that lying is a common human foible and most people struggle at times with the truth. But establish in the strongest terms what a central part honesty plays in all relationships.

54. ARGUMENTS

Q: How do I handle the frequent arguments I have with my teen?

SON: I'm so angry that you shouted at me. I did nothing wrong.

MUM: You were rude to me when I asked you to take out the garbage.

SON: I was not rude. I did nothing wrong. I'm innocent and you're just being mean.

MUM: You are always rude. You never listen to me. You are just a cheeky so-and-so...

SON: I am not. Stop shouting at me.

Although many of the causes of parent-teen quarrels are teenage behaviours, often parents don't see their own behaviour. They don't perceive their sarcastic or belittling manner. Both sides compete for the position of who is the most wronged and the interaction reels out of control. Although easier said than done, we should ideally aim to move away from this pattern of power struggle towards a method of constructive engagement, a dialogue in which each party demonstrates respect, acknowledges emotions and truly listens to the other. The reality is that the parent is the one who will have to role model this kind of behaviour and hope with time that the teen learns to engage appropriately too. But when both are spinning out of control, nothing is gained.

Nevertheless, the reality is that regular quarrelling is normal and not all that harmful. Dr Terri Apter, researcher and lecturer at Cambridge University and author of *You don't really know me*, explains: 'What my research, reassuringly, shows is that quarrelling with your teen doesn't necessarily mean you have a bad relationship. The quality of a parent/ teen bond has several measures: ...the willingness to share a range of daily experiences and to express a range of feelings – happiness as well as their unhappiness. Some parents and teens who engage in frequent arguments have, by these measures, a good relationship.'

WHAT TO DO:

- When you need to bring up a conflictual topic, don't start with accusations or attacks. Immediately you put their back up and you will get nowhere.
- Start from the position of 'I': 'I would like to try to sort this out'; 'I am sorry we had that disagreement.'
- Avoid 'always' and 'never'.
- Avoid sarcasm.
- Avoid ridiculing and belittling.
- Try to avoid catastrophising.
- Allow him to speak and genuinely listen without interrupting with 'yes, but…'.
- Your aim is to provide direction and improvement to your teen, not to win a power struggle.
- Use paced respiration: breathe in for four seconds, hold for four seconds and breathe out for four seconds. Repeat four times until you feel yourself cooling down.
- Be the parent, not the child. Responding to argumentative slings reinforces the conflict and keeps everyone in an emotionally flooded state.
- To stop an escalating quarrel, simply stop talking.
- Keep it short and keep focused on the core issue.
- Do not bring up every misdemeanour of the past. It has no value and is destructive.
- Acknowledge your child's responses and when they are reasonable, recognise them as such.
- Remember, this is not about who is right or wrong, or who wins or loses. The objective is to guide your child or direct her to a new behaviour.
- Don't hesitate to apologise for any bad behaviour on your part (for example, swearing, losing your temper, being wrong).

55. SELF-CENTREDNESS

Q: My daughter is so self-centred! Help, what can I do?

MUM: Hurry up and come downstairs or you'll miss the school bus.

DAUGHTER: I can't manage to fix my hair. It's such a mess!

MUM: I'm packing all your books into your bag for you so you don't miss the bus! You should've packed them last night.

DAUGHTER: I look terrible. I can't get my hair right. Please pack my sports gear too.

MUM: Get away from the mirror and hurry up!

The term used by developmental psychologists to describe this behaviour is 'egocentricism', which means the centre of my world is me. As parents, we see this as selfish but it is a normal developmental stage. 'Self-absorbed, preoccupied and wound up in themselves, living in "all about me" bubbles' is a totally normal thing for adolescents between 12 and 14, says Laura Kastner. She explains that adolescents' higher-level brain is still under construction. What we as parents see as selfishness, thoughtlessness or irrationality is often inattentiveness rather than outright defiance and disobedience.

Adolescents are preoccupied with their 'new' bodies, their iPod playlists, their pimples and their friends. Kastner explains that 'teens will grow out of egocentricism, especially if parents play their cards right by avoiding power struggles, which make teens keep up their resistance to parents' controlling ways'. By about 15 or 16, they usually begin to see things less myopically and have a broader perspective, and hence their behaviour shifts. As parents, we may become exasperated at this self-centredness. We may also become morally incensed. The good news is that it is not necessarily a sign of 'bad character' but a normal feature of adolescence.

WHAT TO DO

- Attempt to stay calm and not get incensed by this behaviour.
- Make the point and keep it simple and brief.

- Allow them to suffer the consequences of their self-absorption (like missing the bus or a lift).
- Limit your response to a few short sentences and leave out words such as 'thoughtless', 'selfish' and 'brat'.

56. CONFRONTATION

Q: Why does he challenge everything that is important to us?

DAD: Davey, have you decided what course you are applying for?

SON: I think university studies are a waste of time.

DAD: But you haven't even begun to fill out your application.

SON: I don't really care! What do I need it for?

DAD: It's so important for your future.

SON: I've got my guitar and I just want to play music anyway.

Most of the battles and confrontations with parents are due to normal teenage development. The important areas of sexuality, religion, politics and careers are often the points of conflict with parents. In order to reach adulthood as an autonomous well-developed self, it is necessary for teenagers to pull away from parental control and our value system. Too easily we get drawn into battles and confrontations that are harmless. Often our teen is just testing the waters. It is worth saving the non-negotiable rules for significant issues. Decide what those issues are and make everything else negotiable and open for discussion.

Dr Jennifer Wyatt, psychologist and co-author of *Getting to calm*, explains that 'teens sift through the leanings of their parents and peers as well as the ideas around them, ultimately arriving at their own set of values in their twenties'. They move away from their parents' identities and then tend to migrate back to the values they were brought up with. Numerous studies reveal that teens do indeed take on the trends of their peer group for a while, but they are unlikely to totally abandon the ethics ingrained in the family. They may experiment with risky behaviour but most teens remain steadfast in terms of the core values related to right and wrong.

- Understand that challenging your views and values is part of a teenager's construction of a new independent self.
- Trying to control his views or values means you will never succeed.
- Control what you can control – your own emotional responses.
- Give him the space to challenge you. Don't bash his beliefs.
- The bad attitude that is often part of confrontation is mostly related to hormones, brain development and the need to pull away from his parents.

57. ANGRY TEENS

Q: How do I handle an angry teen?

MUM: Don't think you can get away with that kind of behaviour.

SON: Leave me alone. I hate you all!

'There are few things as hard to withstand as hostility from one's own child. It hurts. But when adults manage to stay adult even when under attack, they often end up with more influence than they thought they had,' explains Marie Hartwell-Walker, professor of psychology at the University of Massachusetts and author of *Tending the family heart*. In the vast majority of instances, an isolated episode of anger displayed by an adolescent is a reflection of their immature and possibly bratty self. When the anger and hostility are unrelenting, however, there is something deeper going on. 'Parents need to try to uncover the genesis or root of the anger,' recommends psychotherapist Serenne Kaplan. 'Don't panic in response to the behaviours, let your teen know that you have noticed he is in pain and struggling,' she counsels.

Anger is quite often a sign of depression, deep sadness or fear. Teenagers' anger often seems totally out of proportion to their reality. If you have treated your child with a measure of love and respect, and that child is still hostile, it may have very little to do with you or how that child was raised. There are more influences on a child's life than his or her parents. The teen's hostility may become unbearable. It may spiral down into threats from both sides. The teen threatens to leave; the parents threaten to kick the kid out. Both parties are just plain scared. 'Believe it or not, the intensity of feelings can be a hopeful sign,' says Hartwell-Walker. Where there are fights, there is still room to salvage the relationships. Hartwell-Walker recommends the following steps:

WHAT TO DO:

- Hang in there. Parental tenacity is required. Continue to express love and concern, and stubbornly refuse to give up.
- Take the anger seriously, but not personally. Don't take each and

134

every issue as a personal attack. There are many influences other than yours on your child's life.

- Get professional guidance in the form of a counsellor.
- If it is an ongoing problem, it is essential to get a therapist to assess and intervene. There could be underlying issues, such as psychological reasons or biochemical depression.
- Apologise if there is something to apologise for. It's never too late to rectify a difficult relationship. An honest apology can shift you all to a better place.
- Allow your kid space to realise that he has gone too far. Give him a way to back down gracefully.
- Remember that your teen is as scared as you are: hostile moods are often covers for fear.

58. FAILING

Q: What do I do if my teen is failing?

SON: If you just got off my back, it would be much better.

DAD: What would be much better?

SON: You drive me crazy telling me to do my work and it makes it worse. I would do fine if you left me alone!

'Here is one thing not to do,' emphasises Dr Anthony Wolf, author of *Get out of my life*. 'Do not back off teenagers who do not adequately do their school work.' Although there are as many different approaches to this problem as there are experts, Wolf explains how he changed his approach dramatically. He used to advise parents whose kids were failing or not doing school work to leave them alone and allow them to get poor grades or even fail. He reasoned that this would possibly motivate them to change their behaviours. How else would they ever learn to take responsibility?

His experience, however, revealed that these kids often just kept on failing. He now strongly advises parents to step in when kids cannot get their act together with school work. His experience, supported by much data, reveals that appropriate parental involvement does produce better results. You may ask the question, if I do get involved, how will he ever learn to take responsibility? Maybe he will and maybe he won't, but you are getting him into the habit of doing some work and that is better than being in the habit of doing nothing.

WHAT TO DO:

- Remain aware of what is happening with your teen's school work. You don't need to hover like helicopter parents (see page 90), but don't wait until the end of the school term to find out what has gone wrong.
- Although you want your teen to take responsibility for his school work and grades, if he is failing then step in.

- Try to determine whether any extraneous factors may be contributing, such as depression, binge drinking, marijuana use or bullying.
- If you suspect that he is depressed or abusing substances, speak to your GP and make an appointment with a professional counsellor or psychologist.

59. POOR GRADES

Q: What should I do if my teen is getting poor grades at school?

MUM: Have you completed your assignment?

SON: I left my book at school.

MUM: Again! What are you going to do?

SON: I'll get an extension and hand it in later. No big deal.

MUM: It is a big deal. You do this all the time!

It is understandably frustrating for parents when a teen does not take school work seriously and is unmotivated. It is a common problem in adolescence, and may simply be a particular stage of maturation or it may manifest a more serious problem. Nevertheless, there are appropriate levels of concern and the more responsible your teen, the less involved you need to be. However, when he repeatedly leaves his books behind, does not hand in work on time and performs poorly in tests, then you may have grounds for unease. But when you find yourself frequently getting worked up, constantly bickering about school and continually lecturing your teen, it can spiral down into a relentless battle, one that 'only the teen can win,' lament Foster Cline and Jim Fay, authors of *Parenting with love and logic*. Instead, it may be time to explore a little deeper as to whether this is just a case of laziness, lack of motivation, a phase in his life or a more fundamental problem.

There are numerous possible causes for poor school performance, the most common of which may include too high expectations on the parents' part, the child's absorption in other interests, learning disorders, depression and anxiety, peer pressure or substance abuse. Each one of these requires a different approach.

WHAT TO DO:

- You cannot push a teen to study or succeed.
- Have a chat to the teacher, school mentor or principal to gain insight into what is happening at school.

- This may be a developmental stage so encourage your child, and observe his general behaviour for a while.
- If the problem persists, it is worth checking out whether the following apply:
  - » If you suspect he is depressed, or possibly abusing substances, get advice from an experienced counsellor. (See 'Depression' on page 158.)
  - » If you suspect this could be a learning disorder, arrange for a competent professional assessment. Ask the school or your GP for advice.

60. MOTIVATING TEENS

Q: How do I motivate my unmotivated teen?

DAD: How about doing your homework?

SON: I'm just taking a break. Maybe I'll do some later.

DAD: Why don't you just finish it now?

SON: I'm really tired. It's only due in a few days.

DAD: Didn't you say you wanted to work harder this term?

SON: Dad, please leave me alone.

Parents of adolescents frequently complain about how unmotivated their kids are. Teens don't have any problems with motivation. They are in fact extremely motivated. They are motivated to go to the movies, go to a party, shop, upload the coolest stuff onto Facebook, text their friends, skateboard, surf and play the guitar. 'Social success…is much more important to teens than academic success,' says Australian parenting expert Michael Grose.

Motivation itself is not really the problem. It is school work that may pose a problem. A common feature in teens is an apparent lack of motivation with regard to school work. Yet many teens really do want to succeed. Sometimes it is a maturity issue and once they have shifted through a particular stage, they seem to improve. The two types of motivation are often called intrinsic motivation, or doing something that has a greater goal, and extrinsic motivation, or doing something that brings a reward. Intrinsic motivation is more profound and long-lasting, whereas extrinsic motivation usually dies after the reward is achieved. Grose explains that there is also a vast difference between the genders. Girls are inherently more motivated, more diligent and generally much tougher on themselves than boys.

WHAT TO DO:

- Try to instil the value of persistence and not quitting. Encourage your children throughout their early years to always complete a programme or project. Do not allow them to quit when it gets a little tough. A major cause of lack of motivation is that they lose interest or are unable to finish when the going gets a little difficult.

- Encourage goal setting, particularly short-term, achievable goals.
- Support and promote things that they are really good at. Nothing is as motivating as success.
- Ensure they get sufficient sleep. Most teens today are chronically sleep deprived and this impacts dramatically on their learning and behaviour.

61. REBELLION

Q: How seriously should I take my child's rebellious nature?

MUM: What is that disgusting thing doing in your eyebrow? Get it out before your dad comes home!

SON: Oh, come on, Mum! It's just a ring.

MUM: Are you crazy? You look ridiculous. What next? Piercings all over?! You are going off the rails.

It is important to determine whether what you are experiencing with your child as adolescent rebellion is destructive or genuinely harmless. Some experts distinguish between healthy and unhealthy rebellion. Expressions of identity, such as weird haircuts, strange clothing styles and, yes, even body piercings, are usually quite harmless, however bizarre and daunting for parents.

Rebellion is one of the ways in which teens proclaim to their parents: 'I am not you' or broadcast to the world: 'I am different.' If adolescents have been given choices and a fair amount of personal control and space to express themselves, they have probably established a healthy sense of independence from their parents. Such kids often don't go through a rebellious stage at all, explains Serenne Kaplan. The research shows that both extremes of parenting, the hovering helicopter parent as well as the hyper-disciplinarian sergeant-major type, will most likely lead to some form of rebellion. The good news is that with a loving, insightful parent, your kid will get through the phase with time. When a teen 'rebels' in a single area but is generally responsible in other areas of life, there is usually very little to worry about, explains Foster Cline. It is appropriate to express your distaste without any major conflict. However, if the rebellious behaviour is self-destructive it is certainly not right to simply accept it. Signs of more serious or unhealthy rebellion include associated bitterness and rage, and contempt for all authority figures. Although you cannot control your child, you need to express your disapproval in the strongest terms. Even though teens on the road to independence and adulthood don't need approval, they most definitely still want acceptance.

- Practise loving and consistent discipline from an early stage.
- Attempt to understand the reason for the rebellion.
- In the midst of a rebellion, keep focused on the issue.
- If it is simply harmless rebellion, express your distaste (if you must) and let it go.
- In the case of more serious, destructive rebelliousness, try to avoid confrontation. Direct confrontation never works with teenagers. On the contrary, it makes them more rebellious and more willing to push their parents' limits.
- When communicating, begin by 'editing out' a vast amount of what you feel. Try to keep your indignation and outrage out of the discussion. The emotion incites their anger and you want them to have some clarity so they can see what they did was wrong.
- If you lecture, they feel accused and defensive, and fight back.
- Do not bring up every misdemeanour of the past. It has no value and is destructive.
- Acknowledge your child's responses and when they are reasonable, recognise this.
- Remember that this is not about who is right and who is wrong, or who wins or loses. The aim is to direct your child and encourage him to shift to a new behaviour.
- Consider professional help if you feel stuck.

62. TEENS AND DRIVING

Q: Is it appropriate for me to be concerned about my teenager driving?

MUM: Drive safely, Jamie.

JAMIE: Don't worry, Mum! Let's go, guys. We're in a hurry!

MUM: Stop right there! Let's go back to our discussion on safe driving...

JAMIE: Okay, Mum... No drinking and driving, no fooling around, no speeding, no rushing.

The number one cause of death in adolescents is motor-vehicle accidents. So it is entirely appropriate that parents should be concerned about teenagers beginning to drive. Being behind the wheel on his own is thrilling for your teenager, and spine-chilling for you. It is a great privilege and a huge responsibility for a teen to take his place behind the wheel. But it's a parent's responsibility to spell out the real dangers of driving. Usually alcohol is added to the mix of teens and cars. But even without alcohol, an adolescent's lack of insight together with fearlessness and risk-taking will be enough to contribute to the potential for road accidents.

Our teens do need our guidance and caution regarding the hazards of driving. Obviously they will need to go through the process of learning to drive, possibly doing a safety course and getting some lessons before obtaining their driver's licence, but even once they are permitted to drive alone, stipulate the guidelines and always encourage safe driving.

WHAT TO DO:

- Emphasise to your teen that driving is a life-and-death issue.
- If you buy a car for your teen, it is best to get a used older car.
- Share the details of motor insurance and the issues of liability with your teen.

- Implement accountability and consequences for recklessness and possible damage, such as sharing the costs of excess damage payments should they be responsible for a car accident.
- Remind them of the dangers intermittently (without nagging).

63. BULLYING

Q: What can parents do about teenage bullying?

DAUGHTER: I'm not going to school!

MUM: You can't stay away again.

DAUGHTER: I hate school!

MUM: Is someone bullying you or being nasty? Just ignore it and walk away.

DAUGHTER: You don't understand anything!

Parents and teachers often don't understand just how extreme bullying may become or how far-reaching the damage can be. It is a problem that affects millions of schoolchildren globally, who wake up every day afraid to go to school. It's not only those kids who 'don't fit in' who get bullied. Teens may be targeted just for who they are, how they look, their race, their style, where they come from, their sexuality, how much money they have or don't have, or even for excelling at something. 'Bullies don't have to be emotionally disturbed or come from bad families. They look like any normal kid, which makes it so much harder for their parents and educators to see or acknowledge the behaviour,' explains Rosalind Wiseman, bullying expert, American parenting educator and author of *New York Times* bestseller, *Queen bees and wannabees*.

Physical bullying may include tripping, punching or hitting their target. Verbal bullying with taunting and teasing may be slightly different from psychological bullying, which involves excluding or gossiping about kids. Verbal bullying extends to cruel text messages and internet posts, described as 'cyberbullying' (see 'Cyberbullying' on page 215). One of the most painful aspects of bullying is that it is relentless and can cause a teen to remain in a state of constant fear. There is no stereotypical bully and both boys and girls can be bullies. They may be outgoing and aggressive or appear reserved on the surface. CNN commissioned University of California sociologists Dr Robert Faris and Dr Diane Felmlee to conduct a study, which examined the dynamics and root causes of bullying. The result is one of the most important studies ever conducted on bullying and aggression. The findings make it easier to understand why targets and bystanders are so reluctant to ask parents for help. For the target, exposing the bullying means admitting your vulnerability and that people, even friends, don't like you. For the bystanders, those who observe the bullying, things are just as awkward. When they see someone in their group being turned on, the most common reactions are to do nothing or, even worse, join in. They don't want to be associated with the target and risk being humiliated or shut out as well.

We need to guide our children on how to take appropriate action as a bystander and not collude. Many disagree and say we can't or shouldn't micro-manage children's behaviour – we should just let the kids work it out. But working it out never happens. The bully, or the child who has more social power, always 'works it out' to their advantage, explain the researchers.

Wiseman suggests that some of the standard approaches and protocols regarding bullying should be revised. She suggests that ignoring the bully often just gives him more power, and telling our kids to 'develop new friends' or that 'bullies are weak and insecure' is often totally ineffectual. She has suggested the following approaches, which have been adopted by the Obama Commission on Bullying:

- Take bullying very seriously.
- Teens who are bullied often feel helpless and desperate. Hoping the problem will go away doesn't work. Your teen can be helped by developing a strategy and a support system.
- Help your teen to follow this approach:
  » The moment bullying happens, breathe. Observe who is around. Breathe again.
  » If you can, find the courage to say 'Stop!'. You can simply say to the bully, 'Stop pushing me into the lockers' or 'Stop sending those disgusting text messages'. Hold your head up high and do not cower.
  » Always try to walk towards safety – not necessarily just away from the bully. Walk towards a classroom where you can see a

teacher or mentor you trust. If you are outdoors at a sports field or park, walk towards the coach or a group of adults.

» Avoid hitting back or threatening to retaliate. This often leads to an intensification of the bullying.

» Report the bullying. It is always the right thing to do. Report the bullying to an adult that you trust to help you through the problem. Be specific about the bullying behaviour, where you are when it occurs and what you need to feel safe.

» If you are being bullied online, refer to the section 'Cyberbullying' on page 215.

EMOTIONS AND CRISES

IT IS A FRIGHTENING EXPERIENCE for a parent to cope with an emotionally distressed child. We feel our child's pain more acutely than our own. We feel helpless and sometimes even responsible for their stress, mood dysfunction, depression or crisis.

This chapter examines the normal mood swings and emotional flooding experienced by adolescents. It is bewildering for parents to observe the extreme mood fluctuations in their teenager. Scientists have found that the mechanism normally used by the brain to calm itself down in stressful situations seems to work in the opposite way in teenagers. Helpful strategies on how to stay calm and defuse emotional turmoil are suggested. This chapter also looks at when parents need to be concerned about a teen's distress and seek professional help.

Most teenagers will experience depressed moods at some time or other. It is completely normal and common during adolescence to feel depressed intermittently, and more so than during other life stages. However, 'there is cause for concern if he is in a depressed state most of the time,' explains Professor Garry Walter, chair of adolescent psychiatry at the University of Sydney. A crisis for a child at any time is significant, but somehow for teens, it is compounded by the concomitant adolescent emotional surges. There are many small crises in teenagers' lives, including school and exam pressures, difficult friendships and tumultuous relationships. Many teens also suffer as a result of major crises, enduring the divorce or illness of their parents, eating disorders, substance abuse, severe depression and anxiety, even suicidal thoughts. We need to take these issues very seriously and provide a great deal of support. In some cases, counselling may be necessary.

64. EMOTIONAL FLOODING ......

Q: Why do I just 'lose it' with my teenager?

SON: Mum, I'm going out.

MUM: No you're not.

SON: Yes, I am.

MUM: I said you are not going out until you have finished your homework.

SON: I've had enough.

MUM: Don't be rude to me! In fact you are downright rude and insolent! And I can't stand your obnoxious behaviour! And your @#$% room is a mess! And you are @#$% impossible...

. . . .

On occasion for some, and often for others, teens will be defiant. They will also be lazy and messy and offensive and unappreciative. It is easy to become enraged with a teen, but it is also highly ineffective, explain Drs Laura Kastner and Jennifer Wyatt, authors of *Getting to calm: Cool-headed strategies for parenting teens*.

Unbridled anger is an extremely disabling emotion. When we are in the midst of conflict, intense emotions are unleashed. Kastner calls this 'emotional flooding'. During this aroused state, adrenalin is released, the heart rate rises and stress hormones are released, resulting in sweating, flushing and raised blood pressure. This is identical to our flight-fight reaction in response to danger. As we are flooded with emotion, a constructive conversation is impossible. This is because the brain activity shifts from a 'thinking brain' (prefrontal cortex activity), which controls clear thinking, problem solving and achieving perspective, to the emotional centres of the brain (amygdala) and we make threatening, exaggerated, distorted remarks. This is the process that occurs in a typical parent-teen confrontation. The developing teenage brain reacts emotionally to almost everything, and when we as parents are upset, emotional flooding occurs as we also regress into a primitive brain state.

Kastner and Wyatt advise following the 'calm' technique in order to avoid emotional flooding and help prevent you losing control.

WHAT TO DO:

Say the word c-a-l-m to yourself as you follow these four steps:

- C – Cool down. Try to control yourself without trying to control anyone else.
- A – Assess options. Determine what the best approach may be in this instance. Ask yourself whether it may be better to postpone the discussion until everyone has calmed down or whether it is possible to continue the conversation.
- L – Listen with empathy. Do not interrupt. No ifs, no buts.
- M – Make a plan. Consider ways of moving forward; devise a strategy.

65. STRESSED OUT

Q: How do I handle my teen's stress when I too am suffering from stress?

MUM: How was school today?

DAUGHTER: There's too much work! And I have my music exam next week and I have netball and athletics this afternoon. And Sarah has been so nasty to me all day.

MUM: Just try to take it easy.

DAUGHTER: What are you talking about? You don't understand one bit how stressed I am.

Stress is endemic. Life in this fast-paced electronic age is demanding. We feel overextended and overwhelmed, constantly trying to attain the elusive work-life balance as we juggle our work commitments with our parenting. And what often escapes us is that teenagers' lives can be just as stressful. Not all stress is bad for us though. Parents and kids alike need the challenge of work, goals and vision to keep us motivated and focused. Unfortunately, this positive type of stress is stretched beyond its value and most of us live with overwhelming and damaging negative stress. And this sort of stress is not merely a mental state – it also manifests itself in undeniable physical effects. Stress is one of the most significant triggers for burnout and depression.

Coupled with the stress, anxiety and agitation you may be feeling, knowing your teen is stressed makes you feel even worse. Your communication and relationship with each other may also feel strained. How to manage your own stress while trying to focus on helping your teen manage hers, isn't easy, but it is important. Your adolescent is at a vulnerable point in her life. As she searches to establish her identity, she feels pressure coming at her from several angles, including social, family and school. You can help your teen keep calm and learn to cope by trying to ensure that home is a happy and safe space. This means working on yourself, and your own stress and emotional wellbeing.

Her ability to de-stress begins with you: she looks to you as her most significant role model to learn effective strategies to cope.

WHAT TO DO:

- Focus on your own stress-management techniques. Learn how to meditate, do yoga or practise mindfulness. It is of value to read up on the practice of mindfulness, a very effective tool in managing stress.
- Encourage your teen to learn a stress-management technique, such as breathing exercises.
- Find something you and your teen both enjoy and can do together to relax – take a walk, swim some laps, go out for a drink. When you take a break together, it's an opportunity to build your relation-ship, but at the same time you are also teaching another lesson: how to relax.
- Encourage your teen to get plenty of exercise. It's a great stress buster.
- Don't underestimate the power of sleep. Adolescent expert Michael Grose emphasises that sleep deprivation is one of the major causes of many adolescent problems, including poor school performance and moodiness.
- If you feel like your or your teen's stress is just too much, talk to someone – it is important to seek professional counselling.

66. MOOD SWINGS

Q: Is it normal for my teenager to experience such huge mood swings?

MUM: What's wrong with you?

SON: Nothing.

MUM: You're in a bad mood again.

SON: No, I'm not!

MUM: Just snap out of it! It's enough.

SON: Leave me alone!

It is bewildering for parents to observe the extreme mood fluctuations in their teenager. But rest assured that, for the most part, mood swings are quite typical of adolescence. They are an unavoidable side effect of the dramatic physical, hormonal and brain transformations taking place. Recent ground-breaking research demonstrates that teenagers' petulant behaviour and mood swings are due to unexpected chemical reactions in their developing brain. Scientists have found that the mechanism normally used by the brain to calm itself down in stressful situations, seems to work in the opposite way in teenagers, explains Dr Sheryl Smith of the State University of New York. The effect of these changes is that whatever the teenage person's reaction to stress is likely to be, whether it is to cry or be angry, the reaction will be amplified. 'While to adults it may seem like an overreaction, to the teenager it is the only thing they can do,' say the researchers.

This study is thought to be the first to suggest an underlying physiological, as opposed to a behavioural-psychological, explanation for teenage mood swings. You may well be concerned as to whether the mood swings are more serious than other adolescent changes. But unless your teen's angry, depressed or anxious mood continues over an extended period of time, there is no reason to be overly concerned.

- Don't interrogate your teen by firing off questions like, 'What's wrong with you?' They don't know what's wrong.
- Instead, acknowledge that you can see they are having a hard time and make yourself available to talk.
- If they don't want to talk, back off and allow home to be a safe, comfortable and non-judgemental environment.
- Your teen's bad mood usually has nothing to do with you. But it is worth establishing this by asking, 'Are you angry or upset with me?'

67. SCHOOL PRESSURE

Q: Is it normal for my teen to feel anxiety or foreboding about school?

MOTHER: What's so bad about Sunday evening?

SON: Every Sunday I have the same sinking feeling, and Sunday night is the worst time of the week. That feeling is with me when I wake up on Monday morning and doesn't go away until school starts.

MOTHER: And what about once you're at school?

SON: Once I'm at school, it's fine, although there is always pressure.

For many teenagers, most of whom are not unhappy, every Sunday brings with it a sense of unease, anxiety and apprehension. The thought of another week of school ahead can feel ominous. There is no doubt that high school is not a particularly fun experience for teenagers, particularly the final year or two. There may be wonderful times – school camps, sports and cultural events, socialising and special occasions, and just hanging out with friends – but most teenagers, whether motivated or not, feel the pressure and expectations associated with high school. The overt message that they receive is that performing well at high school is crucial: 'you'd better buck up and start working', or 'you are not working hard enough', or 'you could do better', or 'don't you realise that this is so important for your future?'

The response to this varies dramatically from teen to teen. For some, the egging on may motivate them, but for many it just pushes them further away. The pressure of school and the need to perform are real and this pressure is constant through the higher grades. It does get overwhelming at times. Dr Anthony Wolf, author and adolescent expert, believes that it is a problem. But not necessarily a bad problem. He goes as far as stating that 'the problem is that it is necessary for the child to feel some stress'. He explains: 'No, most of the time it isn't fun, but the pressure and the resultant anxiety is what makes people work and the pressure is necessary.' But we need to be on guard in case it becomes overwhelming. If your teen feels anxious a lot of the time, if she can't sleep, if she is feeling depressed and develops physical symptoms, it is important to seek professional attention. But a little bit of healthy anxiety occasionally is okay to get a teenager going.

WHAT TO DO:

- Understand that, up to a point, feeling the load and pressure of school is normal and appropriate.
- Try to create a supporting environment so that home is a comfort zone away from the stresses of school.
- Ascertain whether the stress or pressure has become detrimental. Manifestations such as insomnia, depression, physical symptoms and feeling a sense of unrelenting strain may require seeking professional advice.
- Encourage your teen to get sufficient exercise, to eat well and to get enough sleep.

68. DEPRESSION

Q: How do I know whether my teen is really depressed?

DAD: You seem very down these days, Emma.

DAUGHTER: I don't want to talk about it.

DAD: Sometimes it feels like things are so bad for you that you feel there's no way out.

DAUGHTER: Yip.

DAD: You've been unhappy for a while now.

DAUGHTER: Yeah.

DAD: When I have felt like this, it's really helped me to talk to someone.

Most teenagers experience depressed moods at times. It is completely normal and common during adolescence, more so than at other life stages, to feel depressed intermittently. Your teen may feel low or even depressed about lots of things: love relationships turned sour, difficulties at school, troubles with friends. They feel awful when life just seems to get tough, and they feel overwhelmed and stressed. Sometimes there is no apparent reason. If the depressed mood occurs occasionally and most of the time she feels generally good, there is usually not much to worry about. However there is cause for concern if she is in a depressed state most of the time. There are also signs other than the low mood to watch out for. If she shows a loss of interest in friends and fun activities, becomes angry and irritable, grades start slipping and she generally withdraws, these might be indicators of depression. If she loses her appetite or overeats, has insomnia or sleeps all the time, it is time to seek professional help. Many of these signs might also indicate your child's regular use of marijuana.

If you suspect that your teen is depressed, it is a good idea to approach a mental-health professional or your GP. If your teen talks about wanting to die, take it seriously and seek help immediately (see also

'Suicide' on page 170). Garry Walter believes that there are various ways that parents can assist their depressed teenager. He suggests that 'a parent can keep the GP or counsellor informed about the child's progress, encourage the child to persevere with treatment, try to minimise levels of stress in the family, and be openly hopeful – after all, in the vast majority of cases, the outcome is very good.'

WHAT TO DO:

- Take depression seriously.
- Take action if it is a frequent or constant problem. You will need to seek out the help of a professional. It is probably best to discuss the problem with your GP first.
- Offer unconditional love and concern.
- Teens mostly tend to keep things to themselves but be at hand and receptive to listen if they do want to talk.
- Let them know you are present and available for them without being pushy.
- Support them and encourage them to get help.
- If your teen won't go for help and you are worried, go yourself first and get advice on how best to handle the situation.
- Take seriously any talk about suicide.

69. EATING DISORDERS

Q: What should I do if I suspect my teen has an eating disorder?

MUM: Come and get your dinner, Kelly.

KELLY: I'm not hungry. I'll eat later.

MUM: But you didn't eat lunch.

KELLY: I have eaten. Anyway, I am so fat! Just look at me.

MUM: Kelly, you are skeletal! All I can see are bones.

KELLY: Are you blind? Can't you see how fat I am?

It is not always easy to identify eating disorders, as there is a whole spectrum from very mild to extremely severe conditions. If you suspect your teen has an eating disorder, take it seriously and get professional assistance. The most common conditions are anorexia nervosa and bulimia. Eating disorders require medical attention. Do not ignore the situation and hope it will go away. Remember that not everyone who has an eating disorder is skinny. Some may be overweight, such as those with a condition known as binge-eating disorder.

Although much more common in girls, eating disorders do also occur in teenage boys. People with anorexia have an intense fear of being fat, even though they are underweight; they have a distorted body image and are often in denial of their low-weight problem. With bulimia there is binge eating followed by purging through vomiting or the abuse of diet pills, laxatives, diuretics and enemas – characterised by highly secretive behaviour. There is often depression associated with eating disorders. Garry Walter advises parents to 'maintain an awareness about their teen's diet, general appearance and mood, particularly in light of the secretive nature of eating disorders and the range of serious medical and psychological problems that may ensue'.

- If you suspect that your teen has an eating disorder, be proactive and take it seriously. It won't go away on its own.
- Most people with an eating disorder deny that there is a problem. Often they may also feel ashamed. So be compassionate when expressing your concern.
- Do expect your teen to deny that there is a problem.
- Explain that you want to help. Genuinely listen, do not be judgemental and allow her to talk if she is willing.
- You will probably need to approach her several times. Reassure her that you will get her the best help.
- Let your child know that you are worried and that you care. Even if she denies that there is a problem, or gets upset and does not want to talk about it, it is essential to encourage her to get professional help.

70. OBESITY

Q: What can I do about my very overweight teenager?

DAUGHTER: I just can't stand being like this anymore. My life is so miserable!

MUM: Do you want me to try and help you through this?

Obesity is a major global health crisis. Close to 30 per cent of Australian, South African and British teenagers are overweight, with a significant number suffering from obesity. Compare this proportion with the 1 per cent of teens who suffer from anorexia nervosa or the 6 per cent who suffer from bulimia, and you will realise what a significant problem it is. Overeating and a sedentary lifestyle are the obvious causes, but there is no doubt that some teens are more at risk than others. Emotional eaters and those with a genetic predisposition may put on weight in childhood or adolescence. Living in a household with overweight parents or a home environment conducive to eating a lot and doing little exercise, puts kids at risk.

Many people put their obesity down to hormones and metabolism. However, a genuine metabolic problem, such as thyroid disease, is quite rare. 'A small proportion of underlying hormonal issues such as polycystic ovaries or insulin resistance will also increase the likelihood of weight gain and make fat loss difficult' explains Australian nutritionist Susie Burrel. But mostly it is due to excessive intake of fast food, sugary drinks and a sedentary lifestyle. There are very real emotional reasons for overeating, and it can certainly be an addiction. Medically, the risks of obesity include diabetes, heart disease, infertility and even some types of cancer. And the emotional issues are truly crippling for many teens. Poor self-esteem due to obesity is a heartbreaking situation. These teens can't find nice clothes to wear; they are often excluded from parties and sports teams; they feel uncomfortable eating at school or in public for fear of what others think; they are frequently teased and bullied. And many obese teenagers suffer concomitant depression, which will affect their school performance too.

- Family involvement is one of the main means of preventing and managing obesity.
- Help your teen embark on a healthy lifestyle change with your active participation.
- Start a regular physical activity, such as walking, cycling or hiking. Do this with your teenager or as a family.
- Get rid of the junk food and replace the high-fat, sugar-laden snacks with healthy alternatives and power foods – fruit, vegetables, whole-grain bread.
- Cut back on sugary drinks – they are a major contributor to obesity.
- Engage the professional help of a nutritionist dietician who can empower and motivate your teen to take action now.
- Don't ignore the major emotional issues. Consider seeking the help of a professional therapist to help your teen improve the situation, lose weight and deal with the underlying causes of the overeating.

71. CRISIS

Q: We are in a major crisis with our teen. Help! What do we do?

DAD: I just don't believe it.

SON: I am sorry. I am really sorry.

DAD: You have wiped out the car! How could you drink and drive again?

SON: I don't know what I was thinking!

When a crisis hits the life of our teenager, it tips the family into a downward spiral of anguish, anger, anxiety and guilt. It is extremely traumatic and distressing. We panic and, understandably, think that we have to do something immediately. A crisis with a teen – for example, discovering he is using drugs, a major eating disorder, a diagnosis of severe depression or a car accident – is undoubtedly serious, but rarely an emergency. There is almost always time to seek out the best professional advice as well as guidance from others who have been in a similar situation.

Sometimes what you regard as a crisis, such as discovering drug use or illicit sexual activity, is indeed a very serious issue. But it has probably been going on for some time. What makes it a crisis is that you have just discovered it. You will almost always have time to think and act on it wisely and sensibly. It is also important to remember that crises are nearly always temporary. It rarely gets worse after the crisis – it usually gets better. There is hope for moving on to better times and resolving the situation.

WHAT TO DO:

- Don't panic. Take a deep breath. You need time to think rationally and make decisions about the best course of action. Don't just react, rather consider the options and engage the best plan.
- Seek professional intervention and advice. Talk about the options

with the best person available. This might be your family GP, or a contact at your church or the school, or a mentor.

- Try to avoid blaming and hurling accusations, which will be your impulse in the heat of the moment. There will be time to thrash out all the issues. The peak of the crisis is not the time to do this.
- If this is a repeat of a similar crisis from the past, such as a relapse of drug use (see 'Drug use and teens' on page 187), you may need to take a tough-love approach.

72. DIVORCE

Q: How do I handle my teenager through my divorce?

MUM: How are you feeling about Dad and me getting divorced?

DAUGHTER: It's really bad!

MUM: You know we both love you and always will. But we just cannot get along with each other anymore.

DAUGHTER: I don't want you to get divorced from Dad. This is a disaster for me!

Divorce is an extremely traumatic experience for all involved. In a child's world, and more specifically for teenagers, divorce may feel like a disaster. Unrealistically, children often feel responsible in some way for the marriage break-up. Every teenager and every family is different so it is difficult to predict how a particular teenager will respond to her parents' divorce. However, there are significantly increased risk factors for teens whose parents get divorced. Teens may demonstrate mood swings, withdrawal, problems at school or general defiance.

Divorce is a significant loss for everyone involved. Your teen experiences the loss of a 'normal' family. You should allow her to go through this genuine grieving process while assuring her she is loved by both parents and that support is there for her. 'Teens are often forced to grow up quickly through a divorce,' laments Christopher Hudson, life coach and author of *Parenting clues for the clueless*. 'They may be required to take up extra adult responsibilities, they often unfortunately land up as a confidant and their parents may be unable to provide the previous level of support or nurturing due to depression, leaving the teen to navigate life alone.'

WHAT TO DO:

- Emphasise to your children that the divorce is not in the slightest their fault. They often harbour the feeling of guilt that if only they had behaved better, this wouldn't have happened.
- Be honest about your feelings and situation. This does not mean

you should necessarily share personal details, but honesty about the facts and your emotions always helps.

- Provide someone outside the family for your teen to talk to. Counselling is tremendously valuable.
- Be understanding and compassionate if your teenager acts up during a divorce or shows misconduct. But don't excuse it or allow it to continue long term; it can spiral out of control.
- Do not encourage your teenager to take sides. They need to maintain a good, objective relationship with both parents.
- Do not use your child as a messenger. Communicate directly with your ex-spouse about details regarding your child.
- Do not share your adult/personal problems with your teenage child.
- Maintain family routines as far as possible.

73. PROFESSIONAL HELP

Q: When does one need to seek professional help for an adolescent problem?

MUM: Are you okay? You don't seem yourself these days?

DAUGHTER: Yeah, I'm fine.

MUM: I don't want to pry and push you, but if you aren't feeling right, there is so much we can do about it.

DAUGHTER: It's okay. I'm okay, I suppose.

MUM: It's not your fault you feel awful.

DAUGHTER: Actually, I am feeling awful. It's been going on for a few months now...

Seeking professional help is not admitting failure. It is a bold and courageous step that is often required to give us some guidance as parents during distressing times. Life as a teenager has always been a complex labyrinth. Today more than ever, as parents we may need professional direction to guide us through this. Adolescents themselves do not look for help. 'Young people – particularly boys – tend not to seek professional help when they are in psychological distress. Rather, young people more commonly try to sort out their problems on their own or suffer in silence,' explains Professor Debra Rickwood of the School of Health Sciences at the University of Canberra in Australia.

As parents, it is our responsibility to obtain advice and support when it appears that our teen is in some type of crisis. There are two basic situations that may require us to seek professional help. The first is a sudden, dramatic change in our teen's behaviour or mood. If all of a sudden your son's school performance deteriorates significantly or your daughter's behaviour is completely out of character, professional advice is called for. The second reason is a progressively deteriorating situation regarding conduct, mood or performance over a period of a few months. For example, your child may become very depressed or anxious. Professional care does not necessarily involve long, drawn-out months of counselling sessions. Sometimes one or two effective sessions with a competent therapist may be all that is required to iron out a problem.

WHAT TO DO:

- In order to find a therapist, it is best to get professional recommendations from your family GP, paediatrician or a school counsellor. And enquire among your network of close friends and colleagues about therapists with a good reputation for dealing with adolescent issues.
- When choosing a therapist, there is no harm in seeking out satisfied clients for recommendations.

74. SUICIDE

Q: How seriously must I take it when my daughter says she wants to die?

DAUGHTER: My life is so terrible and I just feel like dying.

DAD: I'm worried about you and I care about you. What do you mean, you feel like dying?

DAUGHTER: I just do.

DAD: Have you seriously thought about suicide?

DAUGHTER: Yes, I have, I feel desperate at times.

Suicide is one of the leading causes of death among teenagers, with the rate of suicide increasing significantly in adolescence. The rates differ between boys and girls. Girls think about and attempt suicide twice as often as boys. Yet four times more boys die by suicide than girls, perhaps because they use more lethal methods. A teen who has suicidal thoughts suffers terrible anguish and despair. Many teens with immobilising depression may learn to put on a happy face, so do be aware of fluctuating moods. South African psychiatrist Dr Shelli Sandler highlights the value of talking openly about the subject: 'Don't be scared to ask your teen directly,' she stresses. 'Ask the question – Are you feeling suicidal? It is absolutely not true that talking about it will give people the idea.' Sandler emphasises that this 'allows you to make some sense of it all and implement an intervention as soon as possible'.

Suicidal thoughts tend to come and go. However, it is important that your child gets help to develop the skills necessary to decrease the likelihood that suicidal thoughts and behaviours will emerge again with the next crisis. In order to try to prevent suicide, early intervention for depression is strongly encouraged and a psychiatrist is best suited to help the family evaluate which of the many treatment possibilities would be most helpful.

All talk about suicide, whether it is during a temper tantrum or an offhand comment, needs to be taken seriously, explains Professor Garry Walter. He advises parents, when talking openly with their teen about whom they are concerned, to ask whether plans have been made to harm herself and to try to persuade the child not to engage in anything self-harming. Parents should also indicate that they love and care about her, underline the benefits of obtaining professional help and offer to accompany the teenager to the doctor or other health professional.

WHAT TO DO:

- Get help immediately. Through your GP or a psychologist, you will need the intervention of a psychiatrist for your teenager.
- Keep an eye on your teen if she seems depressed or withdrawn.
- When someone is threatening suicide or showing alarming signs, the doctor will need to admit your child to hospital for in-patient treatment.
- A team approach is required to evaluate the best treatment options. A specialist psychiatrist will prescribe medication and a variety of psychotherapeutic and counselling approaches.
- Don't diminish or disregard your adolescent's struggles. An issue that might not be a big deal for you can be immense and all-consuming for a teen.

ALCOHOL AND SUBSTANCE ABUSE

ALTHOUGH PARENTS ARE CONFRONTED BY many tough challenges when raising teens, the number-one issue that strikes fear into the heart of a parent is drug abuse. To empower drug-free teens we need to meet this issue head on from early in the teen and pre-teen years. This chapter explores the issues of parental responses to alcohol consumption and drug experimentation. Although responsible alcohol consumption and reckless drug abuse seem like two completely opposite ends of the spectrum, when it comes to adolescence they are often closer than we think. Most teens are not responsible occasional drinkers. Teenagers generally drink to get drunk. Many teens can be labelled as regular binge drinkers, consuming five or more standard drinks in one sitting at least once a week. Many teens also experiment with illegal substances, particularly marijuana, and are more likely to do so while under the influence of alcohol.

As parents, we are often not sure what our stance towards alcohol intake should be. Many of us have a glass of wine, a whisky or a beer occasionally ourselves, and some of us drink regularly, which may persuade us to condone alcohol consumption in teenagers. Few people realise exactly how alcohol wields its power. Anything beyond a single unit a day for women and more than two per day for men starts initiating serious toxic effects. And the effects are far worse in adolescence. 'Few people realise just how deleterious the effect of binge drinking and excessive alcohol intake is on the young brain,' stresses Peter Silbert, clinical professor of neurology at the Royal Perth Hospital, Australia. Therefore, we need to be vigilant about alcohol and substance abuse ourselves and especially for our teens. We must understand the serious dangers posed to our children under the influence and recognise the pernicious damage to the developing brain.

Communication, open discussions, setting boundaries and good role-modelling are the essential tools advocated by the experts, but obviously none of these is infallible.

75. DESTRUCTION FROM ALCOHOL

Q: Other than the danger of drinking and driving, is alcohol really so bad for teens?

DAD: Don't drink too much tonight, Shaun.

SON: I won't, Dad!

DAD: What does that mean?

SON: We just have a few packs of beers and some Jack Daniels. We won't drive. Don't worry.

For teenagers, the effects of a drunken night out may linger long after the hangover wears off. Consider these facts. Teenagers under the influence of alcohol are far more likely to do something that will endanger their lives. Alcohol increases their chances of becoming aggressive, engaging in a physical fight or getting into trouble with the law. Under the influence, they are more likely to smoke marijuana, use prescription medication and harder drugs, and they are significantly more at risk of being involved in a fatal car accident, becoming pregnant or making someone pregnant.

Alcohol has a power of its own. Teenagers, just like adults, vastly underestimate that power and almost always think that they can handle it. Mounting evidence from numerous scientific studies demonstrates how the still-maturing teenage brain (up until at least the age of 21) is particularly susceptible to damage from heavy drinking. A number of recent studies have shown that teenagers who abuse alcohol have problems with memory, learning and other brain functions compared with their peers, and that these effects continue into adulthood. A recent ground-breaking study led by neuroscientist Susan Tapert of the University of California, San Diego in the US, compared brain scans of teenagers who drink heavily with scans of those who don't. Tapert's team found significantly damaged nerve tissue in the brains of those who drink.

Teenagers generally drink to get drunk and many can be classified as regular binge drinkers, consuming five or more standard drinks in one sitting at least once a week. Although some of what you read about the health benefits of moderate alcohol use is true, this doesn't apply to youngsters. Adolescence and moderation are mutually exclusive phenomena.

WHAT TO DO:

- Begin an ongoing conversation about alcohol with your teens in their earlier years.
- Arm them with information but avoid moralising and lecturing – teens are not receptive to lectures.
- Tell them the facts about the dangers of alcohol in as non-judgemental a way as possible. This will probably not stop them from experimenting or drinking but it will certainly influence their decision-making and their internal control in the long term.

76. ALCOHOL DAMAGE IN TEENS: SHORT- AND LONG-TERM EFFECTS

Q: Exactly how does alcohol cause physical and mental damage?

DAD: Please don't drink too much tonight.

DAUGHTER: Oh come on, Dad! It's no big deal. You drink too.

DAD: I don't binge drink. I only have a glass or two of wine at a time.

DAUGHTER: We have a few drinks; it's no big deal.

How much alcohol is okay? How bad is alcohol for teens? Does it cause long-term cognitive damage? Can it kill?

Few people realise exactly how alcohol wields its power. We all know that one or two glasses of wine, especially red, can actually be good for you. It relaxes your blood vessels, lowers your blood pressure and contains antioxidants in the form of resveratrol. But anything more than that starts initiating toxic effects. And although some of what you read about the health benefits of moderate alcohol use is true, this doesn't apply to youngsters.

As alcohol is consumed, it swiftly crosses the blood brain barrier and has a marked effect on cognition and brain function. In the short term, alcohol causes immediate changes. As the blood alcohol concentration rises, euphoria and excitement give way to poor judgement, lack of coordination, aggression, memory disturbances, blurred vision, drowsiness and stupor. If the levels rise even further, coma and death are possible. An excessive amount of alcohol in a single heavy binge may cause death.

In the long term, alcohol is highly addictive and damaging to body and brain. Just about every organ system sustains damage, with the brain and liver bearing the brunt. With regular use and abuse, the teen develops an increased tolerance to alcohol. The raised liver enzymes also mean that he must drink much more to experience the same effects, which leads to more drinking, which may contribute to addiction. The toxic effect of the alcohol means that brain cells in various neurological structures die, thereby reducing the total brain mass. In a young and developing brain, this is disastrous. The brain cells are sensitised and then damaged by the high toxic levels. This makes the drinker very irritable when he is not drinking and sets up craving, which often leads to addiction. On average most addicts have developed their addiction problem by the age of 18. Obviously, most kids don't become addicts or alcoholics, but there is no knowing which of them will get through the phase relatively unscathed and which will deteriorate into a downward spiral of addiction. One of the major problems is that we haven't yet questioned our own attitudes towards alcohol and other mind-altering substances.

WHAT TO DO:

- Adolescence is a time of experimentation. Parents can't necessarily prevent their teenagers from experimenting with alcohol, but they can encourage sensible drinking habits.
- Teach your child sensible approaches, such as how to say no, what the standard drink recommendations are, alternating alcohol with non-alcoholic drinks and not drinking on an empty stomach.

77. HOW AGAINST TEEN DRINKING SHOULD I BE? . . . . .

Q: To what extent should I oppose my teenager drinking?

MUM NO. 1: They are going to drink anyway, so what difference will it make if I forbid it?

MUM NO. 2: I can ask him not to drink, but how much control do I really have?

MUM NO. 3: I suppose all teens drink; it's normal.

DAD NO. 1: I don't really mind, as long as they don't drink and drive.

DAD NO. 2: Youngsters need to have a bit of fun. Boys will be boys.

. . . .

Just how opposed to alcohol should we be? As you can see from the comments above, parents often don't know the answer to this question. Dr Anthony Wolf, author of *I'd listen to my parents if they'd just shut up*, counsels quite the opposite to this laissez-faire approach. He advocates close supervision of teenagers when it comes to alcohol. Know where they are; know what they are doing; and know who they are with. Check up on them. This does not mean they should be micro-managed in all aspects of their lives, as is appropriate with younger children. But don't stand back in this important area and let things take their own course. Supervision has its limits though. A child intent on drinking or using other substances will find a way to do it despite a parent's constant surveillance. The research data also demonstrates that children who don't drink or take drugs do so out of choice, and not because their parental supervision is that much more intense.

So if surveillance is not enough, how can we really have a meaningful influence on their use or abuse of substances? Dr Michael Carr-Gregg, a renowned Australian adolescent psychologist, believes that we can be effective and the way to do it is by talking to our teens. Not just any kind of talking, but honest, open, adult communication. Although the research demonstrates that anti-drinking and anti-drug talks – particularly those delivered in the form of warnings – are totally ignored by teenagers, the real difference we can make is in *how* we talk. Teens, and younger children for that matter, do not respond to lectures. A conversation that is open and genuinely honest is far more effective. Don't necessarily expect that the conversations will stop your teen, but the main impact of talking is that their approach to alcohol and drugs will be more cautious and thoughtful. Wolf believes the value lies not in the lessons they may or may not learn from us, but rather in the absolute frankness of the conversation.

WHAT TO DO:

- You cannot micro-manage your teenager, but do have some level of surveillance. Don't stand back – stay involved.
- Understand the serious dangers posed to your child under the influence of alcohol and what it does to the developing brain.
- Do not lecture your teen on the dangers of alcohol. Instead, have adult conversations with your teenagers regularly. This means an open discussion that is a dialogue rather than a critical sermon.
- Confront your own behaviours and attitudes to alcohol. If you regularly consume excessive amounts, any attempt to influence your child's behaviour will be futile.

78. TEENAGERS' AND PARENTS' VIEWS ON ALCOHOL

Q: What do parents and teens themselves think about alcohol?

DAD: Do you have any idea just how dangerous binge drinking is for your brain?

SON: Ah, Dad! Don't believe everything you read in the papers!

DAD: Seriously, it has a very damaging effect.

SON: Dad, you used to drink too. And you still do.

I recently facilitated a very interesting focus group of 16-year-old Australian teenagers. The issues that emerged seemed to reflect much of the current worldwide data on the behaviours and attitudes of teenagers towards alcohol and drugs. This group of youngsters acknowledged that both alcohol and drugs are easily available to teenagers, including those under age. Although there were some teens who didn't drink at all within this group, the vast majority really liked the effects of alcohol and drank regularly. Most of the teens I spoke to thought that using 'hard drugs' was not a good idea, but saw nothing wrong in using marijuana.

With a similar focus group of the parents of adolescents, the views were also reflective of those universally. The parents were in complete agreement on the outrageously damaging effects of hard drugs. They were mostly against the use of marijuana and binge drinking, but were quite ambivalent in their attitudes to alcohol use in general. They were unsure of just how against it they should be.

Many questions are asked about the role of parental behaviour and its effects on teenage alcohol patterns. There is no doubt that children of alcoholics are at higher risk of addictive behaviour. But what about supposedly 'normal' parental behaviours? What about parents consuming large amounts of alcohol in a recreational way? Children do not do what we say, they do what we do. So when a parent has three or four whiskies at the end of a long day or finishes a bottle or two of wine on the weekend, he gives permission for his teenage son or daughter to binge drink. It is time as parents to confront our own behaviours and attitudes to alcohol and illegal substances.

WHAT TO DO:

- A multi-pronged approach with a combination of supervision, open communication and good role-modelling is ideal.
- Although some parents believe in implementing a zero-tolerance alcohol rule, this is also likely to provoke a rebellious response.
- As parents, we need to be quite clear about our own attitudes to alcohol and alcohol consumption. If you regularly consume excessive amounts of alcohol, any attempt to influence your child's behaviour is futile.

79. DRUNKOREXIA

Q: I have recently heard of the term 'drunkorexia'. Is this a real condition?

MUM: You haven't eaten a thing all day and now you are off with your friends again?

DAUGHTER: I'm not hungry and anyway, we will have a few drinks so maybe I'll eat something later.

MUM: Don't drink on an empty stomach! And anyway, you're drinking too much.

Drunken anorexia, also unofficially known as 'drunkorexia', is the act of skipping meals and cutting out food in order to have more calories for alcohol. Another form of this alarming new trend is when teens decide not to eat while on a drinking binge in order to make vomiting more likely. This means they won't absorb the alcoholic calories. According to researchers at the University of Missouri in the US, there are three times the number of females to males who binge drink without eating in order to lose weight. Alongside the conventional eating disorders, including anorexia and bulimia (see 'Eating disorders' on page 160), one of the 'appeals' of drunkorexia is the appetite-suppressant effect of the alcohol and the fact one ingests fewer calories.

Numerous studies have shown links between eating disorders and alcohol abuse. Up to a third of bulimics have alcohol- or drug-related problems, and 36 per cent of women receiving treatment for alcohol abuse also confess to eating disorders. This fairly new trend of combining starvation and binge drinking puts young women at even higher risk of developing more serious eating disorders, together with alcohol abuse problems. It also poses the danger of alcohol poisoning and chronic diseases in later life. And women are more vulnerable to liver damage and cirrhosis at lower levels of alcohol consumption than men.

WHAT TO DO:

- Alcohol abuse in teens is a frightening reality, but there is always help at hand. Speak to your GP, a counsellor or therapist as soon as possible. It is a painful process for parents to confront, but professional intervention is vital.

- If you are suspicious of alcohol abuse and/or an eating disorder, intervene immediately before things get to a critical level.
- If you suspect your child might be drinking, you may also need to talk to the school. When students are abusing alcohol and other substances, they often skip classes and play truant.

80. MARIJUANA

Q: How worried should I be about marijuana?

DAD: What do you think about marijuana, Ethan? Do lots of kids in your class smoke?

SON: Weed is not addictive, Dad. Everyone knows that.

DAD: Have you ever smoked it?

SON: Only once, Dad. It's not a big deal.

Many teens experiment with illegal substances, particularly marijuana. They tend to vigorously deny its addictive qualities. Many will contend that it doesn't set up a physical craving. But there is no doubt that it is addictive by its power over an individual. In my focus groups with teens, most say they've just tried it once. Don't believe it: far too many teens smoke weed on a regular basis. Disturbingly, there has also been an exponential rise in the use of prescription drugs and other harder drugs, such as cocaine, ice and crack cocaine, among teenagers.

A significant problem with marijuana and teens is that it removes the sense of drive and purpose. Some say it makes them lazy, but in fact it removes the urge to take any action. Users drift in the 'here and now' and couldn't care less about anything. They lose the coping skills necessary to deal with everyday challenges. It is quite normal for teens to feel bored, a little anxious about school or in a low mood intermittently. Marijuana cancels out these feelings.

The marijuana used today is also not the version of 'grass' that people smoked a decade or so ago. Marijuana is far more powerful than it was 20 years ago. The immediate side effects, other than feeling high and happy, include short-term memory loss, lack of concentration and lack of motivation. Long term, it may have far-reaching consequences, including significant mental health problems in adulthood, warns Professor Garry Walter, chair of child and adolescent psychiatry at the University of Sydney. Professor Walter notes that those problems can even be unmasked in adolescence. As with alcohol, marijuana is also particularly detrimental to the developing teenage brain.

Certainly, the vast majority of teens are experimenters and will not go on to become dependent on marijuana. 'Some adolescent health specialists see substance experimenting as inextricably tied into a teenager's life whilst forming an identity, values and self definition,' explains American adolescent psychologist Dr Laura Kastner. She advises that a realistic approach should include health, safety and harm reduction, and entail close supervision and limiting the opportunities for children to dabble with the drug.

WHAT TO DO:

- Good surveillance is essential. Keep track of your teens; know where they are and who they are with.
- Talk to them about marijuana and drugs from an early age.
- Have a conversation, not a lecture. You may wish to initiate discussions about marijuana and drugs by referring to people in the news: talk about celebrities and overdoses, for example.
- Do not make this a taboo subject and simply hope it will never become your problem.
- Seek professional help (in the form of a therapist or GP) if you think your teen has a problem. Consult with your GP or the school counsellor or a therapist to gain some insight and guidance.

81. DRUG USE AND TEENS

Q: How do I keep my teenager away from drugs?

MUM: What do you think of things like smoking weed or experimenting with drugs?

DAUGHTER: Mum, are you crazy? Why are you asking me this? Do you think I would ever do this?

MUM: No, of course not. I know you aren't doing any of this! But it is so important to talk about it.

DAUGHTER: Do we have to?

Communication, open discussions, setting boundaries and good role-modelling are all the essential tools advocated by the experts, but that is not to say they will work.

My own teens have lived through the devastation of a close family member's drug addiction. Observing the havoc wreaked by addiction, and experiencing the family's anguish and despair through rehab and relapses has brought them face to face with a monster they never want to confront. Throughout this heart-wrenching process, everything was openly discussed. They even attended a Narcotics Anonymous group meeting when the family member reached one year of 'clean time'. That meeting introduced them to a group of individuals from every walk of life, some as young as themselves. It also exposed them to the reality of substance abuse and the horrors of addiction that remain hidden behind closed doors.

But without such a jolting family experience, how do we deal with the issue of our teenagers and substance abuse? Two important approaches, explains Australian adolescent expert and author Dr Michael Carr-Gregg, are close supervision and good communication. Although not always effective, supervision and a level of surveillance are essential. Dr Anthony Wolf explains that it does not feel comfortable being open with our teens about such issues, but it is essential. The value lies not in the lessons but in the absolute frankness of the communication itself.

We also need to ask why my teen wants to participate in this type of risky behaviour. Often it is purely adolescent experimentation and the need to have a good time, but when teens actively try to change how they feel it is often because they are struggling to cope with feelings or situations that they aren't able to handle on their own. This behaviour is sometimes referred to as self-medicating, explains Garry Walter – an attempt to feel better or to just change the painful feelings. If you suspect your teen is abusing substances this could be a strong indicator that he is struggling to cope and may need professional help to successfully deal with the reasons behind this risky behaviour.

WHAT TO DO:

- Many experts encourage establishing zero tolerance for drug use; others argue that this may be impossible. Either way, be sure to gather as much information as possible. Do not remain in the dark regarding alcohol and substance abuse.
- Allow your teen to ask questions, and educate yourself on the issues so you are in a position to answer. Find out about drug addiction; know what marijuana does to the body and brain; understand how severe substance abuse is.
- Establish consequences and be firm.
- Check up on your teen. Always know where he is, with whom and when he is returning.
- Be calm when discussing drug-related issues.
- Get to know your teen's friends and their parents.
- Seek professional help. Contact your GP, a counsellor or school mentor if you are concerned.

82. WARNING SIGNS THAT MY TEEN IS ABUSING DRUGS

Q: What do I do if I suspect my teen is abusing drugs?

DAD: I need to talk to you about something extremely important.

SON: What now?

DAD: I will ask you questions but you don't have to answer now. This is very serious. I will try not to get angry. I am with you through this, but we need to get help soon.

It is extremely painful acknowledging that your child may have a drug problem. But if you have a suspicion, act on it immediately. Even though your kid may demonstrate some of the warning signs of drug use, it does not necessarily mean he is abusing drugs. Similar behaviours can be attributed to other causes, such as depression or simply the nature of adolescence. It is understandable that parents may try to attribute these behaviours to something else. Notwithstanding this, do not ignore warning signs of teenage drug abuse. Professor Dan Stein, head of psychiatry at the University of Cape Town, urges those in trouble to seek help and 'help raise the profile of this secret health challenge'.

Inherent in the abuse of and addiction to drugs is intense denial. If at least five of the following signs are present for a period of time, you need to confront your teen and seek professional help as soon as possible:

- Being verbally or physically abusive
- Loss of interest in activities
- Sudden drop in school grades
- Not coming home on time
- Disappearance of money or valuables
- Lying about whereabouts
- Sudden increase in or sudden loss of appetite
- Drastic weight loss
- Constant excuses and 'ducking and diving'
- Finding pipes, rolling papers, glass or plastic vials

- Falling asleep in class
- Defiance or aggression (a sudden change in behaviour)
- Truancy from school
- Being very sleepy
- Always running short of money (or having excessive money)
- Paranoia
- Being very agitated or suddenly hyperactive

WHAT TO DO:

- Try to remain calm.
- Don't dismiss these warning signs. Become more involved and keep a watch on what he is doing, where and with whom.
- You need to speak to your teen but you may first need advice from your family doctor, a professional drug counsellor or a drug help hotline.
- Do not go into denial and hope the problem will go away. Seek help immediately.
- Reassure your teen that you are there for him, but professional help will be needed to get him through this.
- Most teens who are abusing drugs will maintain extreme denial for as long as possible.

SEX AND TEENS

SEX BECOMES A SIGNIFICANT ASPECT of an adolescent's life. Whether we like it or not, many teens begin to engage in sexual behaviour regardless of their parents' moral standpoint. Although many parents avoid talking to their teens about sex, as they feel awkward and ill-equipped, now more than ever teens require responsible and sensible input from their parents. It is best to begin the conversation from early on in your teenager's adolescent years. Your child needs accurate information about sex, but it's just as important to talk about emotions, feelings, attitudes and values. If you are uncomfortable about the subject, don't be afraid to say so. Whatever you do, don't lecture: adolescents almost always tune out of a lecture, particularly about sex and alcohol.

Sexuality is one of the great pleasures of life in a loving and committed relationship. However, with adolescents it can be fraught with many problems. Teens often engage in risky behaviour. They can become pregnant or make someone pregnant; they can contract HIV or a sexually transmitted illness; they can find themselves deeply involved in a relationship that is overwhelming emotionally; they may end up feeling ashamed or embarrassed by the experience; and they may become the victim or perpetrator of sexual aggression and violence. One of the world's best-known parenting educators and author of *Raising boys*, Stephen Biddulph, explains that the more knowledgeable teens are about the risks involved, the less likely they are to engage in risky sexual behaviour. Adolescents today are exposed to a huge amount of sexual material, particularly via the internet, with extremely graphic sexual content and frequently very distorted and aggressive sexual behaviours (see 'Pornography' on page 221). Parents need to counter these misconceptions, and particularly unhealthy sexual messages, with courage and compassion.

This chapter explores many of the issues concerning teenage sexuality and how best to invite open communication. The leading studies on adolescent sexuality show that teens whose parents talk openly about sex are more responsible in their sexual behaviour. The lessons your teen learns today about respect, healthy relationships and what is right and wrong will carry over into their future relationships. This guidance needs to come from you.

83. RISK-TAKING: SEX, DRUGS AND ROCK 'N' ROLL

Q: What is risky behaviour?

DAD: That athlete who jumped from his hotel room died because he was completely drunk and was at risk for crazy behaviour.

SON: It's pretty sad. He was such a superstar.

Adolescence and risk-taking go hand in hand. This is because teenagers need to explore their own limits as well as their parents' boundaries. Risk-taking is part of their path to adulthood and independence. It is also a by-product of peer pressure, raging hormones and a developing brain struggling with impulse control. The problem is they often go too far, and that's why parental support and guidance are important throughout adolescence. Unsafe sex, binge drinking and illegal drug taking are the most common problems associated with risky behaviours in teens. Teenagers like to have fun, but not regular fun – they really like to take risks. It's not just that they use alcohol (often illegally and below the age limit), but that they binge drink. They don't just engage in sexual activity, they often get very risky about their sexual behaviour. They also experiment with illegal substances and drugs, and this is often taken to an extreme.

Obviously, not all teens engage in this kind of behaviour, but many do and therefore as parents of teens we need to confront the problem, as it exists for all of us. However, the nature of adolescence is such that a tough, authoritarian approach, and enforcing strict rules and bans will usually backfire. Educating teens about risky behaviours, such as unsafe sex and binge drinking, should begin to take place long before they reach adolescence.

WHAT TO DO:

- Keep the lines of communication open and make these subjects a major part of family discussions while your children are growing up.
- Be a good role model. If your child is aware of you speeding,

drinking excessively or being aggressive, you've got no chance of influencing him because you are applying double standards.

- Stay involved in their lives and keep an eye on what they are up to.
- Encourage 'safe' risk-taking or channelling of their risk-taking tendencies. Sports like rock climbing, martial arts, canoeing or mountain biking can supply plenty of adrenalin thrills.
- Help your child learn to assess risk. Talk about other people's behaviour and the consequences. (If he hadn't been speeding, he wouldn't have lost his licence. Now he may lose his job as well. And so on.)
- Parenting expert Michael Grose advises parents to minimise risky behaviour by 'staying in the game'. In other words, stay involved in their lives; take an interest in their interests; talk to them about their friends; drive them to places, and so on.

84. 'THAT' CONVERSATION: TALKING TO TEENS ABOUT SEX

Q: How do you talk to teenagers about sex?

MUM: It seems like you and Kevin are really quite serious and happy together?

DAUGHTER: We are pretty serious, I suppose.

MUM: I don't want to be nosy, but just wondering whether you've thought about or discussed sex?

DAUGHTER: Yes, kind of.

MUM: You know my concerns for you and thoughts on sex before marriage.

DAUGHTER: I don't feel like discussing this now, Mum.

Sex and parents do not mix. And yet, sex education is a parent's responsibility. Don't leave it up to the school. Understandably, teenagers do not want to share anything about their own sexuality or sexual life with their parents. And parents are uneasy about their sweet young offspring transforming into sexual beings.

The most important aspect of dealing with sexuality is having the conversation. Talk to your teens about sex and let them know they can talk to you if they want to. Talking is not really about trying to stop them. It is more about arming them with as much information as possible so they can make informed decisions. This is one subject where saying nothing doesn't apply. Remember, talking is not the same as lecturing. This is not the time to judge and moralise. Although there is no doubt that kids today are exposed to much more explicit sexual information via the internet and media than ever before, they really don't seem to know as much as we may think they know about certain important aspects. So that conversation is essential.

Many countries have a comprehensive sex-education programme in high school. However, Dr Michael Carr-Gregg, an Australian adolescent psychologist, affirms that 'many of our young people are ill-equipped to process the sexualised images which bombard them on billboards, the internet, music video clips and TV'. In South Africa, where HIV and Aids remain a huge problem, teens still engage in extremely risky sex. Although schools do offer sex education, children still need strong direction from their parents.

It is an uncomfortable conversation for some parents and an awkward conversation for all teens. The important thing is to just do it. Have that conversation.

WHAT TO DO:

- Begin the conversation about sex with teens from early on in their teen years.
- Be honest. If you're uncomfortable, don't be afraid to say so but explain that it's important to keep talking.
- Be direct. Clearly state your opinion on specific matters, such as intercourse and oral sex. Explain that oral sex isn't a risk-free alternative to intercourse. Present the physical risks objectively, including sexually transmitted infections, unplanned pregnancies, as well as the potential emotional distress with failed relationships.
- Respect your teen's point of view. Don't lecture or try to use scare tactics to discourage sexual activity. Instead, listen carefully.
- Get beyond the facts. Your child needs accurate information about sex, but it's just as important to talk about emotions, feelings, attitudes and values. Examine questions of ethics and responsibility in the context of your personal or religious beliefs.
- Invite more discussion. Let your teen know you are always willing to talk about sex whenever he or she has questions or concerns.
- Stress the importance of safe sex, and make sure your teen understands how to obtain and use contraception.

85. TALKING TO DAUGHTERS ABOUT SEX

Q: How should I talk to my daughter about sex?

MUM: So, would you want to plan for it, or are you going to just let it happen?

DAUGHTER: I'd like to plan for it.

MUM: Well, that is good thinking. Can we talk a little bit about contraception?

DAUGHTER: Maybe in a while. Not now.

MUM: I know you will consider this carefully. You know you can ask me anything and we can talk about it when you feel like it.

DAUGHTER: Thanks, Mum, I know.

We need to prepare our daughters for the stage in their lives when sexual activity becomes a real possibility. Whether your opinions come from a religious, moral or personal perspective, and regardless of whether the overriding message is 'don't do it', or 'wait till you are married' or 'it's fine with me' – begin the conversation. By having the conversation, or several conversations, we can help our daughters make better decisions for themselves. This can empower them to say no, have more control over their sex lives (at whatever stage it may begin) and avoid ever becoming a victim. They can learn from us that sex is a choice they make, not something that should ever just 'happen' to them.

Girls and boys may sit in class together and perform equally well in exams. They may hold the stage in drama as equals, perform in the debating team or on the athletics track with equal prowess, but when it comes to sexual activity there is an imbalance of power. Of course, not all adolescent boys are inconsiderate and sexual predators, but with raging hormones and immaturity – several of them are. (And let's not forget that girls too may be inconsiderate and insensitive.) It is often more comfortable for a mother to talk to her teenage daughters, but there is huge value for the father to be involved in the discussion.

Teach your daughter about contraception. Do not leave this to the school sex-education programme.

Finally, it is a myth that if you teach your children about contraception, they are more likely to engage in sexual activity because they feel they have your permission. This is not the case in reality.

- Have a conversation with your daughter. This conversation can deliver these important messages:
  » Think about how far you want to go long before you are in the situation.
  » Sex will not necessarily secure your relationship.
  » For adolescent boys, sex is seldom a private affair. It is something that is shared very openly with friends, even more so in this world of Facebook and Twitter. Think about this carefully before you engage in sexual activity.
  » With alcohol on board, the probability of having sex is significantly higher. If you get drunk or even just have a few drinks, your capacity to say no will be diminished.
  » Avoid being in a situation alone with a guy when you are drinking.
  » Often sex is just a physical thing for a guy and when it's over, all it means is that he thinks he can have sex with you again.
  » It may feel intimate at the time but for the guy those feelings do pass after the activity.
  » If he hurts you in any way, get rid of him immediately and *do not* keep it to yourself. Tell your parents or a trusted adult.
- Do discuss contraception with your daughter. This is a parent's responsibility, so don't leave it to sex education at school.

86. TALKING TO SONS ABOUT SEX

Q: How should I talk to my son about sex?

DAD: Can we have a chat about things?

SON: Dad, come on, I'm not five years old.

DAD: I know, but there are important things that I want to discuss with you about sex.

SON: Whatever, but really I already know about all that stuff!

The truth is they don't really know it all and much of what they do know is misinformation and possibly distorted. As with daughters and mothers, speaking to sons about sex is often more comfortable when it comes from the dad. However, there are no rules and there is no reason that the mum shouldn't have this conversation if you and your son are reasonably at ease. However, talking about the importance of showing a girl consideration and respect often holds more weight coming from the father or a male mentor. Unfortunately, most dads think that a sex talk with their son means telling them to use condoms. Condoms are essential, but a discussion about being respectful and considerate seldom takes place. As boys become sexually aware, the overriding message they receive via the media is that it's cool to 'hit on' as many girls as possible and it is normal for boys to do wild things. Boys need to hear some very strong messages from their parents too. You may be thinking, 'What will this talk achieve? He won't listen to me!' And you may be correct. He may or may not agree with you at the time. But your words will get into his head and if he hears it more than once, even more so. If you say nothing, however, there is no chance of wielding any influence. By talking about being considerate and respectful to women (especially coming from the dad), your son will internalise these ideas and they may influence his thoughts, decisions and actions.

- Have a conversation with your son. This conversation can deliver these important messages:
  » No means no. When a girl says no, it means no.
  » It is never okay to have sex with a girl who is drunk. It is a case of abusive behaviour by taking advantage of her limited capacity to say no.
  » Any sexual activity is a private matter not to be discussed with friends.
  » It is never okay to have sex without a condom.
  » Feelings and emotions are important.
  » A loving, committed relationship has value.
- Discuss contraception. Your son needs the facts on the risk of pregnancy, sexually transmitted infections and HIV. These issues are the parents' area of responsibility. Don't leave it to the school sex-education classes.
- Use each opportunity to share your value system but don't turn it into a moralising lecture.
- There is no right way to have this talk, and although it's awkward, it doesn't really matter – the important thing is that it opens channels of communication. The more you talk, the better.

87. THE TOUGH TOPICS FOR PARENTS

Q: If I talk to my teen about sex, won't it just encourage her to do it?

DAD: Do you have any questions you would like to ask me about sex?

DAUGHTER: Are you mad? No!

DAD: Well if you do, let me know.

DAUGHTER: Thanks, Dad.

Sexuality is one of those topics that many parents dread talking about. Bear in mind that these are some of the myths and misconceptions that parents live with:

- I don't need to talk about sex until there is a serious boyfriend on the scene.
- If I talk to my teen about sex, it will put the idea in his head.
- Once I've had the talk, that's it, it's done.

'The data couldn't be clearer,' explains Dr Laura Kastner, co-author of *Getting to calm*. 'Children whose parents talk with them about sex have no increased rate of sexuality. And when they do become active, they're more responsible about practising safe sex.' It is also important to commit to an ongoing dialogue through the different stages of adolescence into adulthood. Furthermore, don't worry if your teen won't talk. It's appropriate for teens to hold back on sharing information with parents, particularly regarding sex. It is up to you to raise the tough topics, such as pornography (page 221), date violence (page 203) and homosexuality (page 119). But not all at the same time! Take it slowly.

WHAT TO DO:

- Don't interrogate and don't lecture.
- Don't criticise and try to show them they are wrong. This discus-

sion is not about right and wrong. It's more about safe sex and emotional maturity.

- Make it comfortable for your teen to talk, but don't force her to talk.
- If your teen doesn't ask any questions, it is a good idea for you to convey these messages:
  - » Peer pressure steers many teens into early sexual activity. It takes courage to say no.
  - » If you say no, it means no. No one should have sex out of a sense of obligation or fear. Any form of forced sex is rape, whether the perpetrator is a stranger or your boyfriend.
  - » There is no rush and it's okay to wait. Sexual activity is great in a long-term, committed, loving, strong relationship. In the meantime, there are many other ways to express affection.
  - » Loneliness is another unfortunate factor that pushes some teens into early sex. However, it just leaves one much lonelier. Instead, deal with the loneliness through counselling, support and compassion.

88. DATING VIOLENCE: PREVENTING SEXUAL AGGRESSION AND SEXUAL ABUSE

Q: How do I ensure my son is never sexually abusive?

DAD: Can we talk?

SON: Sure.

DAD: I want to chat to you about responsible sexual behaviour.

SON: Oh please, Dad! Do you have to?

Dr Anthony Wolf, author of five books on parenting, suggests that in addition to talking about being respectful and considerate, there is another important conversation to have with boys, and this should take place on another occasion: sexual abuse. Wolf explains that many teenage boys can be abusive to their girlfriends. Obviously, most are not and no parent would like to even think that their sons may be abusive. However, often the boys who are abusive do not even realise that their behaviour is abusive. They may think that either their behaviour is not abusive, or even worse, that it is acceptable. Therefore, all boys need to hear this discussion. Teens and adults alike are often unaware of how commonly dating violence occurs, so it is important to know the facts and share them with your teen.

Parents should also be alert to warning signs that a teen may be a victim of dating violence. These may include displays of anxiety or fear around their dating partner; suspicious bruises, scratches or other injuries; or excusing their boyfriend's behaviour. Victims of such violence may also show signs of avoiding other friends and loss of interest in school and other activities.

Even though this may well not apply to your son, share these points with him and he may share them with others:

- Many boys are abusive and although I do not think you are abusive, I need to talk to you about what abuse is.
- It is never okay to hit or grab a girl.
- If a girl starts threatening you or hits or kicks you, move away immediately. Violence towards a girl in self-defence is not okay. Just move away.
- If you get into an argument and you are standing very close, move away and leave.
- Do not get into an argument if you are drunk or have been drinking. Once again, move away from the point of potential conflict.
- Don't have sex with a girl who is drunk. This may seem like fun but is a serious breach of her trust and the antithesis of decent behaviour.
- Use of force is never acceptable. It is a most serious case of abuse or rape.
- Don't use verbal put-downs. People may think it's funny to call a girl fat or an idiot. It's abusive. Don't make verbal threats either.
- If she is being nasty or rude, move away and exit the situation.

TEENS AND THE INTERNET – SCREENAGERS

PARENTS BEMOAN THAT THEIR TEENS are constantly hooked up to an electronic universe via numerous devices. The never-ending nature of teenage internet activity drives many parents insane. What a waste of time, they feel. It interferes with school work and their children's personal development. Parents also feel powerless and out of control. Many may even feel a sense of doom and gloom. But is it all bad news? The digital generation to which our teens belong has never known a life before the digital era. Because of it, they can multi-task and make decisions faster. They are accustomed to receiving and processing vast amounts of information all at the same time.

However, there are very real dangers lurking in cyberspace that parents and teens need to be aware of – cyberbullies, pornography and online predators, to name a few. This chapter addresses these issues head on and provides parents with the tools to understand and monitor these dangers. There is certainly a place for parental controls, but most importantly we need to upskill ourselves in order to empower our teens and demonstrate how best to navigate this world safely. In order to do this, we need to dive in and understand how it all works.

Just like teenagers of previous generations, digital-age teenagers relish being connected to and communicating with their peers. Internet technology provides a connection to a universe of people and teenagers derive pleasure from being invisibly in contact with many people. Obviously, this must be monitored for age appropriateness and security. Although it is more difficult for us than for previous generations, as parents we are still the gatekeepers. But rather than adopting punitive measures, begin to participate and guide them (especially younger teens) in this digital world. It is a world in which business, the media and the immediate future lie. Nevertheless, have confidence in your authority – establish internet-free times and lay down the ground rules and boundaries.

89. PLUGGED IN ALL DAY

Q: She's plugged in to the internet all day. What can I do?

No Facebook until you've finished your homework, shouts Mum down the passage.

The moment my boys get home from school, they do a quick check on Facebook. Alex turns on some music on his PC. Ned switches on his iPod and the earphones are inserted for the afternoon. 'No Facebook now. Finish your homework…'

Before I even get to the end of the sentence, I realise how stupid these words are.

'But Mum, I am getting the maths solutions from Brad via Facebook.'

The reality is that any time they are not at school our teens are hooked up to an electronic universe via various devices. Some are even connected during school. This is partly a good thing. They have access to a world of information, which, although no longer in book form, requires them to search and summarise, and develop skills relevant to the world they are living in. It is remarkable how adept our kids are at navigating the electronic world, and are able to deal with such a wide variety of incoming stimuli.

Unfortunately, it is also partly not a good thing. Although they are able to deal with the magnitude of information and multiple stimuli, they now also need that extreme level of stimulation to keep themselves engaged and entertained. They are accustomed to a high-intensity and fast-paced barrage of words, images and videos. They have less tolerance of a slower paced or singular linear activity. This may have seriously contributed to a generation of hyperactive, attention-deficient young teens.

There are also many dangers lurking in cyberspace that parents and teens need to be aware of.

WHAT TO DO:

• Limit the hours they spend online. This is particularly important with younger teens who cannot set their own boundaries. You may need to spell out how many hours each day can be spent on Facebook, video games and the internet.

- Create a short period of time during the day that is digital free. This could be dinner time or a period in the day to catch up. Be realistic in your expectations – if you are reasonable about it, they will generally comply.
- Be aware that, as with all teen compliance issues, they may do it begrudgingly. As with any form of discipline you impose, you need to persist.
- Insist on at least one type of extramural sports activity outside of school per season. This will ensure that a few hours a week are spent outdoors and engaged in physical activity.

90. THE VALUE IN BEING CONNECTED

Q: What could possibly be good about all this electronic connectivity?

HOW U 2DAY?

GOOD N U?

WANT 2 COME OVER LATER?

NO, I HAVE MUSIC @ SCHOOL

AH NO!

K, SIYA LATER

The texting and WhatsApp, BlackBerry and Facebook messaging go on incessantly in the lives of teens. The interminable nature of it and the apparent waste of time drive parents insane. It interferes with their school work and their personal development. It means so much less family time together, as they don't want to be part of family activities.

This may all be true. But is this generation really all that worse off than teens of previous generations? The technology provides them with a connection to an invisible universe of people. What did our generation do when we were teens? We spoke for hours and hours on the phone. Don't you remember driving your parents crazy as you sat curled up with the phone attached to your ear for three hours? Although many of your child's friends on Facebook are peripheral, there are also numerous closer friends in contact through social media. Teens thrive on being connected to their peer group, keeping up to date with what's happening and being able to communicate regularly with mates. Teens also have a real fear of missing out. Instant messaging ensures they are always updated.

All this connectivity provides a medium for not feeling alone. There is of course a flip side, which is that it is important for young people to develop some tolerance for being alone. Being able to tolerate aloneness is an important life skill, and it is different from loneliness. We don't want children to feel lonely but it is important that our teens are comfortable with themselves in the absence of numerous distractions.

- Begin to try to understand and accept that this is the nature of their world and although we may be a step or two behind them, the digital age is our world too. Embrace the positive nature of it.
- Be clear about establishing some electronic-free time in the day, when we are unplugged and engaged in some real 'face time' (as opposed to Facebook time).
- Establish this as a rule, not a request. Insist on it, don't back down and they will realise you are serious.

91. PARENTAL CONTROLS

Q: How much surveillance of my child's internet activity is appropriate?

DAUGHTER: It's so wrong that you are constantly looking over my shoulder checking out what I'm doing.

MUM: But we're just concerned for your own good.

DAUGHTER: Yeah, but don't I deserve some privacy?

MUM: You do deserve privacy, but you also deserve to be protected from predators, cyberbullies, violence and obscenity.

The big question debated by adolescent specialists is just how much internet surveillance is appropriate. To what extent do we need to know what teens are doing online in order to steer them in the right direction and keep them from harm? It is a difficult question to answer and depends on a number of factors, including the particular child, their age and your parenting style. Some parents are comfortable to give their children more independence; others feel the need to keep a tight rein.

The drawback of close surveillance is that your child will not learn to take responsibility for bad choices. Often the need to know exactly what's going on within a teenager's world is a parent control issue and reflects the parents' need to free themselves from worry. Dr Wendy Grolnick, author of *The psychology of parental control*, argues that attempting to control a child's behaviours, attitudes and beliefs will not produce as successful a set of results as the alternative approach, which she terms 'autonomy support'. This involves providing structure and rules but at the same time autonomy for the teen to develop self-reliance and their own moral code.

It is appropriate and necessary to implement some strong ground rules and if for you this means some online parental control measures, it is an effective approach as long as you are open about it. Secret surveillance, such as tracking your child's online activities without his knowledge, is plain snooping. It is dishonest, and although you may feel that you are doing it for your child's good, it is a serious betrayal.

The negative message you are giving your child is that in the adult world dishonesty and betrayal are acceptable as long as you have a good reason to do it.

- Establish some firm ground rules. These should be age dependent. Pre-teens and young teens need much more supervision than older children.
- Encourage internet use in an open, public space, particularly in the case of younger teens.
- Be honest with your children and if you are going to use internet parental controls, let your kids know they are in place. This itself is a deterrent.
- Website blockers may be useful. Although kids can get round some of them, most work well. Internet Explorer has a free parental control option that you can activate.
- Many of the computer security packages that keep your PC free of viruses have a simple online safety section that allows you to block websites that contain violence, gambling, cults, weapons and pornography.
- Make your views on social networking sites and chat rooms clear. If you don't want your child to use them, say so. If you do permit them, establish rules.
- The basic rules should include not communicating directly with strangers, not trading personal information online and not posting very personal pictures or videos online.

92. ONLINE PREDATORS . . . .

Q: What online dangers should we be really worried about?

MUM: There are people out there on the internet who could be dangerous.

DAD: They are not who they say they are.

MUM: Never meet with anyone in person whom you may have met online.

DAD: Don't give any personal information about yourself – your address, your school, your contact numbers – to anyone online.

. . . .

As a parent, you should have no hesitation about repeating this explicit warning. Parents have a number of real concerns about their kids and the internet. As discussed in this chapter, spending a lot of time online may interfere with children's school work, sleep and family activities. But one of the most seriously troubling issues is online sexual predators. Hopefully, your child will never have any contact with a predator over the internet, but these depraved individuals are out there. This is one area where teens need to be taught not to trust. Older teens have usually developed a level of internet savvy. They generally know not to trust anyone over the internet. But, unfortunately, younger teens are still naive and unaware of the vast and dangerous nature of cyberspace. They need to be advised and warned repeatedly never to give personal information, such as addresses and contact numbers, online. All adolescents should be made aware that any entry made or sent electronically may become part of a permanent record that could be used against them in the future. Privacy matters need to be a permanent part of their internet consciousness. Remember, any written words or images have the capacity to come back and haunt you.

WHAT TO DO:

* Be proactive with your children about internet dangers. Have a clear set of guidelines for them regarding internet usage.

- Warn them repeatedly never to meet in person anyone they have met online.
- Warn them never to give personal information to anyone online.
- Warn them to only accept people they know personally as friends on Facebook or other social-media sites.

93. CYBERBULLYING

Q: How serious is cyberbullying?

DAUGHTER: Bella posted something so mean about me on Facebook and now everyone is talking about it. All the girls that I thought were my friends are acting and looking at me funny. I'm not going to school tomorrow. I'm never going back to school.

A post on Facebook or a text message containing nastiness or gossip has far-reaching and significantly damaging repercussions for kids. Cyberbullying, a serious offence, is defined as sending messages or images that humiliate, embarrass or threaten a child or teen via the internet, a mobile phone or digital technology. (In the case of adults, it is not called cyberbullying but rather cyber-harassment, and it is a serious crime.) Often teens engage in cyberbullying in retaliation for an insult or out of boredom. Some are simply power hungry, like the old-fashioned school-yard bully.

But often teens do this because they just think it is funny, and have absolutely no understanding of the scale of damage it can cause. In many instances, teens who have been cyberbullied don't tell their parents. They feel ashamed and often keep it a secret. They think they can handle it or they worry that parental involvement will make it worse. Another reason, explains Emily Moore, a clinical psychologist based in Albuquerque, New Mexico, is that 'they feel that Mum and Dad will pull the plug on computer privileges'. Moore explains that this is a tactic that won't work well: 'It'd be like taking away the keys to the car and saying to your kid, "You're never going to drive."' Although you may feel as though there is nothing you can do to comfort her, just by being sympathetic and present with her through the crisis is supportive – if she reveals the bullying to you, that is. It is valuable to remind your teens about cyberbullying every so often and encourage them to let you know if it happens. I strongly recommend assuring them that they will not get into trouble for what they tell you.

215

WHAT TO DO:

- Take up any instance of cyberbullying with the school, teacher or individuals concerned.
- Make it perfectly clear to your teenager how harmful cyberbullying is. It is a serious act of misconduct and reveals very bad character.
- Encourage your children to tell you about any nastiness they may experience.
- Cultivate in your family an atmosphere of open communication about all issues, including difficult ones and taboos. This may influence your child's decision to talk to you when she's suffering or in trouble.
- Be there for her; listen to what has happened.

94. WHEN YOUR TEEN IS THE PERPETRATOR

Q: What if my kid is not the victim but the cyberbully?

PARENT: 'We recently discovered several instances of my son actually being the cyberbully. The transcripts were unbelievably obscene and I am devastated. I have had numerous talks with him about the severity of this issue, but I don't really understand what to do from there.'

Letter to the *New York Times*, 29 June 2010

It is extremely difficult for parents to acknowledge that their child is a bully. Although it is a painful thing for a parent to discover, the worst disservice you can do your child is not to acknowledge and deal with it in the strongest terms. In response to this reader's letter, Elizabeth K. Englander, professor of psychology and director of the Massachusetts Aggression Reduction Centre, Boston, praises the parent for admitting and accepting the problem: 'Most parents who, faced with the evidence to the contrary, continue to insist that their own children are totally blameless,' laments Englander. 'You are already more than halfway there, simply by virtue of your willingness to accept that your son made a mistake, and that you are the adult responsible for responding appropriately and ensuring that his mistake doesn't happen again.'

Englander's research has found that children are significantly more willing to type very shocking things than say them directly to someone's face. The fact that these communications occur in texts and online greatly reduces their *perceived* impact. 'Kids believe that online statements simply "don't count" because they're not being said to someone's face,' she explains. When a perpetrator is discovered, she urges prohibiting their use of social media and technological communications for a while, but highlights the need for the child to earn his way back to these privileges by demonstrating consistently that he understands the rules and why they are important. He should spend time researching real cases of bullycide – how and why victims of cyberbullying have

217

committed suicide. He should regain access to the internet and mobile phone in stages and only with full parental surveillance. He should only be online with parental-control software that lets you see everything he types without exception, and have significant limits imposed on the time he can spend online.

WHAT TO DO :

- To help prevent a problem arising, assume that any child may become a perpetrator. Spell out to your teen exactly what actions and words are out of line. This is where they require significant guidance. They need to be told that it is just as bad, and possibly worse, to post or text something nasty as to say it face to face. Give them direction along these lines:

  » You may not say anything hurtful to or about anyone.
  » You may not say anything that will embarrass someone.
  » You may not send or receive any pictures of yourself, or anybody else, naked or of a sexual nature. This is considered child pornography and is a serious offence.
  » You may not send or receive messages that describe any sexual behaviour.
  » Once a message or post has been sent, it is not private.
  » Cyberbullying is cruel, serious and a grave offence.

95. BULLYCIDE

Q: Is there really such a term as 'bullycide'?

'She was new and she was from a different country, and she didn't really know the school very well. I think that's probably one reason why they chose Phoebe. A16-year-old student said she had not known Phoebe Prince personally but had heard stories spread about her in the hallways. The investigation found that students abused her in the school library, the lunch room and the hallways, and threw canned drink at her as she walked home. Her sister found her hanging from a stairwell at home.'

('Six students charged for classmate's death, Massachusetts, 30 March 2010', *New York Times Online*, 30 March 2010, http://www.nytimes. com/2010/03/30/us/30bully.html, accessed 15 July 2012)

Jumping off the GW bridge – sorry.

This Facebook status was the last anyone heard from Tyler Clementi, an 18-year-old student at Rutgers University, New Jersey, before he committed suicide after his roommate used a computer webcam to secretly tape and broadcast him kissing another man. (http://fairfieldmirror.com /2010/11/03/%E2%80%9Cbullycide%E2%80%9D-a-sadly-new-pandemic, accessed 15 July 2012)

'Bullycide.' It is hard to believe such a term exists, this hybrid of 'bullying' and 'suicide'. Yet it's a real phenomenon. The person (often a teen) feels so humiliated that she feels she cannot face the world. This may be brought on by a post or message that has gone out digitally, but ultimately it becomes so painful that the teen may feel that killing herself is the only way out. And a child takes her life as a result of being bullied.

Because she is now a teenager and supposedly grown up, she feels it is unacceptable to rely on her parents. She feels the last thing she can do is share this humiliation with them. She may feel so desperate and alone that there is no hope of a future after something terrible has gone live via the internet or into the online world so that everyone knows about it. The only hope in such a situation is if she can feel some level of connection to you as her parent. You cannot take away the pain but you can be there with her through this. The problem is that she has to be willing to tell you about it. She may keep pushing you away with 'you don't understand, you're not helping'. This is true – you may not understand or be helpful, but you are with her in this.

There is no specific profile of the type of teen who is more at risk for suicide as a result of bullying. In her book *Bullycide in America*, Brenda High tells the stories of mothers of children who have committed suicide as a result of being bullied. Their stories are all different, yet the commonality is that the bullying these children endured resulted in suicide. We do know that there is a connection between being bullied and depression, and we know that depression is a risk factor for attempting suicide. Parents and teachers should therefore look for signs that a child is experiencing symptoms of depression, but this is not always the case in victims of bullying.

WHAT TO DO:

- Don't walk away from the problem if you are worried about your child. Whatever you do, stay present and connected.
- She will push you away and tell you she is fine and doesn't need your involvement, but stay involved and keep on talking about the issue.
- Parents and teachers *must* intervene when they see bullying or suspect it is taking place online.
- Watch out for signs and symptoms of depression.

96. PORNOGRAPHY

Q: What can I do about the massive amount of porn that my young teen is able to access?

MUM: What were you checking out on the computer last night?

SON: Nothing much. Just some Facebook posts.

MUM: You are 13 years old and you have been looking at sick porn sites!

SON: Why are you snooping on me?

MUM: I wasn't snooping, the website popped up. I am shocked!

When this fictitious mother stumbled across the website her son had been browsing, she searched his browsing history and discovered pornography beyond her imagination. Her sweet boy had been exposed to the horrors of whips, obscenely huge body parts and positions that were abhorrent to her. Although her husband might try to reassure her that boys will be boys, reminding her that the previous generation used to read *Playboy* magazine instead of going online to access internet porn, what we are dealing with today is different. In the past it was surreptitious and a guy would have to hide his pornographic magazine or wait until the house was empty to try to secretly watch a video. Today teens have unlimited access to free porn anywhere, any time, as long as they have a smartphone.

The average age of Australian and American children's first exposure to pornography today is 11, and most have experienced it by the age of 15. So kids are often viewing porn before they have even had their first kiss. 'Porn sex is also not real sex, it is extreme,' explains Mia Freedman, social commentator and publisher of Mamamia.com.au. Anal sex features in almost all mainstream pornography. Women are paid twice as much for engaging in anal sex as for regular sex in porn scenes. 'Almost 90% of scenes in best-selling porn include physical aggression,' according to porn researcher Maree Crabbe. As a result, porn gives people, especially teens, 'really unhealthy messages' about what women enjoy and how they should be treated during sex. And most of those viewers are teens who haven't even had sex yet. This may consequently become their 'mental hard drive', as they have no other frame of reference.

WHAT TO DO:

- Although traditionally, sex discussions in the family are gender based – mums speak to daughters and dads to sons – it is a good idea for both parents to express their views to give your teenager more than one perspective.
- Both parents need to acknowledge their son's natural curiosity about sex and to reaffirm positive messages of sexuality and intimacy for future healthy relationships.
- It is worth using parent control and net filters on home computers, but be aware that smartphones don't allow for such filters.
- It is parents' responsibility to have continual conversations with their children about sex. These chats need to be age appropriate, but awkward as it may be, honest education in this area is crucial.

97. VIDEO-GAME OBSESSION . . . .

Q: Is my son addicted to violent video games?

DAD: Get off your computer now and come for dinner!

SON: I don't want dinner. I'm in the middle of a game.

DAD: Shut it down now!

SON: I can't shut it now, it's the most exciting part – I've almost killed him! I don't want dinner.

Parents may at first feel proud that their loner has developed great computer skills and has made some friends online with whom he is playing games. With time, however, this child may become obsessed with violent online games. This may lead to isolation from the family and a fixation with battle methods. You may notice that he becomes increasingly aggressive with you and his siblings. This may be an extreme example, and it is true that most teens can manage some exposure to violent games without serious consequences, but in some cases it can become a real addiction.

Mark Gregston, US adolescent expert, says, 'I find nothing wrong with most of these games. But some kids and young adults are being consumed by them, and that's where the problem lies.' Teenagers love playing video games because they provide a challenge and an escape. They offer mental and visual stimuli that can transport the 'gamer' into a world removed from reality. During a game the player is in a state of cardiac arousal and experiences a high as adrenalin is released along with a brain chemical called dopamine, which creates a real sense of pleasure. With time, though, older teens may withdraw more from mainstream interactions and engage in violent fantasies. The latest research shows that exposure to violent video games is a direct cause of aggressive behaviour, aggressive thinking and aggressive feelings. Violent video games are thought to have a greater impact on behaviour than television because your child isn't simply watching the bloody warrior, he *is* the bloody warrior. 'I believe that for most kids violent video games won't do anything at all – especially if the game is played only periodically as a pastime. The normal child won't become desensitised to killing people by simply playing "shooter" video games,' explains Gregston.

In most situations there is nothing to worry about, but there are cases where the gamer becomes totally consumed by violent games.

- You don't need to throw the baby out with the bath water by banning video games altogether. There are plenty of good games – sports, motocross, racing and adventure action with no immoral or violent themes.
- If you have a child who is already prone to violent outbursts, hangs out with rough kids, or seems to lack a moral compass, violent games should be avoided.
- Keep an eye on the games your teen is playing. If you find them objectionable, then get rid of them.
- If your teen is overinvolved in video games to an extent that it is consuming his life, disturbing his behaviour and affecting school work, and you can't get him away from them, then treat it like any other addiction. Engage the help of a good psychologist who deals with such addiction.

BIBLIOGRAPHY

A new life stage

Adolescent development. Available at [http://www.headspace.org.au/parents-and-carers/find-information/adolescent-development] (accessed 3 July 2012).

Flexner, W. 2004. *Adolescence*. Sarup & Sons.

Grose, M. 2010. *Thriving! Raising confident kids with confidence, character and resilience*. Bantam Australia.

Hines, G. & Baverstock, A. 2005. *Whatever!* Piatkus Books.

Pre-teens communicating and relationships: In a nutshell. Available at [http://raisingchildren.net.au/articles/preteens_communicating_nutshell.html] (accessed 17 June 2012).

Surviving adolescence. Available at [http://www.rcpsych.ac.uk/survivingadolescence.aspx] (accessed 3 March 2012).

Sylwester, R. 2007. *The adolescent brain: Reaching for autonomy*. Corwin Press.

UNICEF, 2002. *Adolescence: A time that matters*. UNICEF Publishing.

Yurgelun-Todd, D. 2007. Emotional and cognitive changes during adolescence. *Current Opinion in Neurobiology* 17(2): 251–257.

Communication

Barbieri, A. 20 October 2012. Problem solved. Available at [http://www.guardian.co.uk/lifeandstyle/2012/oct/20/annalisa-barbieri-problem-solved-eating] (accessed 21 October 2012).

Biddulph, S. 2003. *Raising boys*. Harper Thorsons.

Biddulph, S. 2010. *The new manhood*. Finch Publishing.

Chester, E. 2002. *Generation why*. Chess Press.

Communicating with your teen: Give up on lectures and advice. Available at [www.life.familyeducation.com/teen/communication/42909.html] (accessed 26 July 2012).

Faber, A. & Mazlish, E. 2012. *How to talk so kids will listen & listen so kids will talk* (updated edition). Scribner.

Grose, M. 2000. *Great ideas for tired parents*. Random House Australia.

Kastner, L. & Wyatt, J. 2009. *Getting to calm: Cool-headed strategies for parenting tweens + teens*. Parentmap Publishers.

Lehman, J. 2012. *Transform your child*. Legacy Publishing Company.

McWilliam, E. Generation Y and Z in our schools – not an easy group to teach.

Available at [http://www.cwaofnsw.org.au/images/Hauffpresentation.pdf] (accessed 23 February 2012).

Osterweil, N. Talking with teens: Tips for better communication. Available at [http://www.webmd.com/parenting/features/better-communication-with-teens] (accessed 12 February 2012).

Wittmer, D. 2011. *The parent's guide to raising a successful child.*

Wolf, A. 2000. *The secret of parenting: How to be in charge of today's kids.* Farrar, Straus and Giroux.

Wolf, A. 2011. *I'd listen to my parents if they'd just shut up.* William Morrow Paperbacks.

Morals, values and rules

Bradley, M.J. 2002. *Yes, your teen is crazy!: Loving your kid without losing your mind.* Harbor Press.

Carr-Greg, M. 2005. *Surviving adolescents: The must-have manual for all parents.* Penguin Australia.

Fay, J. & Cline, F. 2006. *Parenting teens with love and logic.* NavPress Publishing.

Grose, M. 2005. *XYZ: The new rules of generational warfare.* Random House Australia.

Leman, K. 2008. *Have a new kid by Friday.* Baker Publishing.

Leman, K. 2009. *Have a new teenager by Friday.* Baker Publishing.

Robinson, J. & Carroll, J. 2002. Teens value morality, but will bend rules. Available at [http://www.gallup.com/poll/5656/teens-value-morality-will-bend-rules.aspx] (accessed 15 March 2012).

Techniques to set rules and consequences for your teen. Available at [http://life. familyeducation.com/teen/safety/34464.html] (accessed 21 June 2012).

Walsh, D. 2005. *Why do they act that way? A survival guide to the adolescent brain for you and your teen.* Free Press.

Wolf, A. 1996. *It's not fair, Jeremy Spencer's parents let him stay up all night.* Farrar, Straus and Giroux.

The family

Biddulph, S. 1995. *Manhood: An action plan for changing men's lives.* Finch Publishing.

Chua, A. 2011. *Battle hymn of the tiger mother.* Bloomsbury Publishing.

Cline, F. & Fay, J. 2006. *Parenting with love and logic: Teaching children responsibility.* NavPress.

Elkind, D. 2001. *The hurried child: Growing up too fast too soon.* Perseus Publishing.

Fay, J. 1995. *Helicopters, drill sergeants & consultants: Parenting styles and the messages they send.* Love and Logic Press.

Fingerman, K. 2001. *Mothers and their adult daughters: Mixed emotions, enduring bonds.* Prometheus Books, 2001.

Goleman, D. 2009. *Working with emotional intelligence.* Bloomsbury Publishing.

Horvath, T. et al. Introduction to what is an addiction. Available at [http://www. sevencounties.org/poc/view_doc.php?type=doc&id=48328&cn=1408] (accessed 2 May 2012).

Hubbard, S. 10 steps to better parenting. Available at [http://www.kidsdr.com/parenting/10-steps-to-better-parenting] (accessed 3 July 2012).

Kabat-Zinn, J. 1990. *Full catastrophe living*. Delta Trade Paperbacks.

Kauranen Jones, G. 2003. *To hell and back – Healing your way through transition*. Wheatmark.

Krzyzewski, M. & Wilkinson, J. 2012. *Dear Jay, love, Dad: Bud Wilkinson's letters to his son*. University of Oklahoma Press.

Larkin, P. This be the verse. The Poetry Foundation. Available at [http://www.poetryfoundation.org/poem/178055] (accessed 7 August 2012).

Oliver, J. 2010. *How not to f*** them up*. Vermilion.

Pass, J. 2012. The 3 C's of co-dependency. Available at [http://www.teenandfamily-services.org/blog/] (accessed 13 July 2012).

Rosin, H. 2012. Boys on the side. *The Atlantic Magazine*, September. Available at [http://www.theatlantic.com/magazine/archive/2012/09/boys-on-the-side/309062/] (accessed 28 May 2012).

Twenge, J. 2009. *Narcissism epidemic: Living in the age of entitlement*. Simon and Schuster.

Walton, A.G. How to mess up your kids. Available at [http://www.thedoctorwill-seeyounow.com/content/kids/art3388.html] (accessed 17 April 2012).

Warner, J. 2011. No more Mrs nice mum. *New York Times Online*, January 2011. Available at [www.nytimes.com/2011/01/16/magazine/16fob-wwln-t.htm] (accessed 10 March 2012).

Winnicott, D. 1994. *Talking to parents*. Da Capo Press.

Wolf, A. 2002. *Get out of my life, but first could you drive me and Cheryl to the mall?* Farrar, Straus and Giroux.

Friends and relationships

Apter, T. 2005. *You don't really know me*. W.W. Norton.

Campbell, M.A. 2005. Cyber bullying: An old problem in a new guise? *Australian Journal of Guidance and Computing*. 15(1): 68–76.

Carr-Greg, M. 2006. *Princess bitchface syndrome*. e-Penguin Publishing.

Faris, R. & Felmlee, D. 2010. Status struggles: Network centrality and gender segregation in same- and cross-gender aggression. *American Sociological Review*, February.

Farley, T. 2005. *Modern manners: The thinking person's guide to social graces*. W.W. Norton.

Hartwell-Walker, M. 2011. *Tending the family heart* 2nd ed. Psych Central.com Publishers.

Juvonen, J. & Gross, E.F. 2008. Extending the school grounds? Bullying experiences in cyberspace. *Journal of School Health*. 78(9): 496–505. Available at [http://www.cyberbullying.us/bibliography.php] (accessed 26 July 2012).

Kastner, L. & Wyatt, J. 2002. *The launching years: Strategies for parenting from senior year to college life*. Crown Publishing Group.

Keith, S. & Martin, M.E. 2005. Cyber-bullying: Creating a culture of respect in a cyber world. *Reclaiming Children & Youth.* 13(4): 224–228.

La Sala, M. 2010. *Coming out, coming home: Helping families adjust to a gay or lesbian child.* Columbia University Press.

Steinberg, L. & Monahan, K.C. 2011. Adolescents' exposure to sexy media does not hasten the initiation of sexual intercourse. *Developmental Psychology.* 47(2): 562–576.

Wiseman, R. 2002. *Queen bees and wannabees.* Piatkus.

Wolf, A. 2002. *Get out of my life, but first could you drive me and Cheryl to the mall?* Farrar, Straus and Giroux.

Behaviours

Dealing with disrespectful teenage behaviour. Available at http://raisingchildren. net.au/articles/disrespectful_behaviour_teenagers.html/context/1092 (accessed 7 August 2012).

Hayes, E. 2004. Your teen's behaviour. Available at [http://www.bbc.co.uk/health/ physical_health/child_development/teen_discipline.shtml] (accessed 30 June 2012).

Is your teen sexually active? 2007. University of Maryland. Available at [www.health-calculators.org/calculators/teen_sexual_behavior.asp?] (accessed 3 July 2012).

Lareau, A. 2003. *Unequal childhoods: Class, race, and family life.* University of California Press.

Little, E. 2008. *Hard choices: Parenting the adolescent child.* X libris.

Mental disorders. Available at [http://teenmentalhealth.org/understanding-mental-health/mental-disorders/] (accessed 3 August 2012).

Murray, M. 2006. *Freaks, geeks, and cool kids.* Routledge.

Patterns and precursors of adolescent antisocial behaviour. 2002. Available at [www.aifs.gov.au/atp/pubs/reports/cpv/report1.pdf] (accessed 17 March 2012).

Scott-Wooding, G. 2005. *Rage, rebellion and rudeness: Parenting teenagers in the new millennium.* Fitzhenry and Whiteside.

Emotions and crises

Bode, J. 2001. *For better, for worse: A guide to surviving divorce for preteens and their families.* Simon & Schuster.

Caldwell, L. & Tapert, S. 2005 Gender and adolescent alcohol use disorders on bold (blood oxygen level dependent) response to spatial working memory. *Alcohol and Alcoholism.* 40(3): 194–200.

Carr-Greg, M. 2010. *When to really worry.* E-Penguin.

Chambers, R.A. 2008. Drunkorexia. *Journal of Dual Diagnosis.* 4(4).

Cleary, M., Walter, G. & Jackson, D. 2011. Not always smooth sailing: Mental health issues associated with the transition from high school to college. *Issues in Mental Health Nursing.* 32(4): 250–254.

Cohen, T. 2012. Young women skip meals so they can save calories for drinking. *Daily Mail,* 19 July 2012. Available at [http://www.dailymail.co.uk/health/

article-2050486/Drunkorexia-Young-women-skip-meals-save-calories-money-drinking.html] (accessed 27 August 2012).

Dunham, W. 12 March 2007. Hormone turns cute kids into horror teens. Available at [http://www.abc.net.au/science/articles/2007/03/12/1869539.html] (accessed 26 February 2012).

Eckersley, R. 2005. *Well and good: Morality, meaning and happiness* 2nd ed. Melbourne: Text Publishing.

Hudson, C. 1999. *Parenting clues for the clueless.* Promise Press.

Lissau, I. Overweight and obesity epidemic among children. Answer from European countries, 2004. *International Journal of Obesity.* Available at [http://www.nature.com/ijo/journal/v28/n3s/abs/0802822a.html] (accessed 2 June 2012).

Park, A. Teen obesity: Lack of exercise may not be to blame. OnlineTime Health & family, Nov 2009. Available at [http://www.time.com/time/health/article/0,8599,1936777,00.html] (accessed 17 May 2012).

Paturel, A. 2011. How does alcohol affect the teenage brain? *Neurology Now.* 7(6): 23–24, 26–28.

Rickwood, D. 2005. Supporting young people at school with high mental health needs. *Australian Journal of Guidance and Counselling.* 15(2): 137–155.

Rickwood, D., Deane, F.P., Wilson, C.J. & Ciarrochi, J. 2005. Young people's help-seeking for mental health problems. *Australian e-Journal for the Advancement of Mental Health (AeJAMH).* 4(3) supplement.

Soh, N., Touyz, S., Dobbins, T., Surgenor, L., Clarke, S., Kohn, M., Lee, E., Leow, V., Rieger, E., Ung, K. & Walter, G. 2009. Nutrition knowledge in young women with eating disorders in Australia and Singapore: A pilot study. *Australian & New Zealand Journal of Psychiatry.* 43(12): 1178–1184.

Stein, D. et al. 2012. *Textbook of psychiatry,* latest review. Available at [http://en.wikibooks.org/wiki/Textbook_of_Psychiatry] (accessed 10 June 2012).

Walter, G. 2009, *Nessun Dorma* ('None Shall Sleep')? At least not before we digest Treatment of Adolescent Suicide Attempters (TASA). *Journal of the American Academy of Child and Adolescent Psychiatry.* 48: 977–978.

Walter, G. 2012. Suicide is preventable, sometimes. *Australasian Psychiatry.* Available at [http://apy.sagepub.com/content/20/4/271.abstract] (accessed 8 August 2012).

Alcohol and substance abuse

Bukstein, O.G. 2009. Adolescent substance abuse. In B.J. Sadock et al. (eds), *Kaplan and Sadock's comprehensive textbook of psychiatry* 9th ed., vol. 2: 3818–3834. Philadelphia: Lippincott Williams and Wilkins.

Centers for Disease Control and Prevention. 2008. *Youth risk behavior surveillance – United States, 2005.* MMWR, 55 (SS04).

Committee on Substance Abuse, American Academy of Pediatrics. 2005. Tobacco, alcohol, and other drugs: The role of the pediatrician in prevention, identification, and management of substance abuse. *Pediatrics* 115: 816–821. Available at [http://www.pediatrics.org/cgi/content/full/115/3/816] (accessed 19 July 2012).

Gayle, M., Boyd, J.H. & Zucker, R.A. 1995. *Alcohol problems among adolescents.* Routledge.

Griswold, K.S., et al. 2008. Adolescent substance use and abuse: Recognition and management. *American Family Physician.* 77(3): 331–336.

Hopfer, C. & Riggs, P. 2007. Substance use disorders. In A. Martin & F.R. Volkmar (eds), *Lewis's child and adolescent psychiatry* 4th ed.: 615–624. Philadelphia: Lippincott Williams and Wilkins.

How to handle teenagers and alcohol, April 2010. Industry Association for Responsible Alcohol Use. Available at [http://www.ara.co.za/news/4/15/How-To-Handle-Teenagers-And-Alcohol] (accessed 17 July 2012).

Jenkins, R.R. & Hoover, A. 2007. Substance abuse. In R.M. Kliegman et al. (eds), *Nelson textbook of pediatrics* 18th ed.: 824–834. Philadelphia: Saunders Elsevier.

Johnston, L.D., et al. 2009. *Monitoring the future national results on adolescent drug use: Overview of key findings, 2008.* NIH Publication No. 09-7401. Bethesda: National Institute on Drug Abuse.

Kaminer, Y. 2008. Adolescent substance abuse. In M. Galanter & H.D. Kleber (eds), *Textbook of substance abuse treatment* 4th ed.: 525–535. Washington, DC: American Psychiatric Publishing.

Monti, P. 2002. *Adolescents, alcohol, and substance abuse: Reaching teens through brief interventions.* Guilford Publications.

Pichler, A. M. 1995. *Alcohol and drug use among youth.* Nova Publishers.

Preventing alcohol-related harm in Australia: A window of opportunity. October 2008. Available at [http://www.health.gov.au/internet/preventativehealth/publishing.nsf/Content/tech-alcohol-toc~tech-alcohol-3~tech-alcohol-3.1] (accessed 12 May 2012).

Sadock, B.J. et al. 2007. Adolescent substance abuse. In *Kaplan and Sadock's synopsis of psychiatry, behavioral sciences/clinical psychiatry* 10th ed.: 1294–1298. Philadelphia: Lippincott Williams and Wilkins.

Schuckit, M.A. 2007. Drug abuse and dependence. In D.C. Dale & D.D. Federman (eds), *ACP Medicine*, section 13, chap. 11. New York: WebMD.

Substance Abuse and Mental Health Services Administration. 2009. *Results from the 2008 National Survey on Drug Use and Health: National findings.* Office of Applied Studies, NSDUH Series H-36, DHHS Publication No. SMA 09–4434. Available at [http://oas.samhsa.gov/nsduh/2k8nsduh/2k8Results.pdf.] (accessed 29 June 2012).

Teen alcohol abuse. Narconon International. Available at [http://www.narconon.org/drug-information/teen-alcohol-abuse.html] (accessed 22 March 2012).

What is teen substance abuse? Available at [http://www.webmd.com/parenting/guide/teen-alcohol-and-drug-abuse-topic-overview] (accessed 13 April 2012).

Sex and teens

Bell, R. 1998. *Changing bodies, changing lives: Expanded third edition: A Book for Teens on Sex.* Crown Publishing Group.

Calabia, A. Why teens start having sex in the first place. Environment, age of partner and perceived family support may affect young people's decisions to have sex. July 2001. Available at [http://www.psychologytoday.com/articles/200107/teens-and-sex] (accessed 24 July 2012).

Changes your child is going through. The Society of Obstetricians and Gynaecologists of Canada. Available at [http://www.sexualityandu.ca/parents/changes_your_child_is_going_through] (accessed 26 June 2012).

Covey, S. 2003. *The 7 habits of highly effective teens*. Running Press Editions.

Grant, I., Atkinson, J.H. & Gouaux, B. 2012. Research on medical marijuana. *American Journal of Psychiatry* 169(10): 1119–1120. DOI: 10.1176.

Haffner, D.W. 2001. *Beyond the big talk: every parent's guide to raising sexually healthy teens – From middle school to high school and beyond*. New York, NY: New Market Press.

Marcovitz, H. 2004. *Teens and sex*. Mason Crest Publishers.

Moore, S. & Rosenthal, D. 2007. *Sexuality in adolescence: Current trends*. Taylor and Francis e-Library.

Pavanel, J. 2003. *The sex book: A no-nonsense guide for teenagers*. Wizard Books.

Sexual risk behavior: HIV, STD, and teen pregnancy prevention. 2011. Available at [http://www.cdc.gov/HealthyYouth/sexualbehaviors/] (accessed 22 July 2012).

Tyson, D. 2012. Sexting teens: Decriminalising young people's sexual practices. Available at [http://theconversation.edu.au/sexting-teens-decriminalising-young-peoples-sexual-practices-8922] (accessed 10 August 2012).

Unmasking sexual con games: Helping teens avoid emotional grooming and dating violence. Boys Town Press.

Witmer, D. Effective communication helps parents deal with tough issues. Available at [http://parentingteens.about.com/od/parentingclasses/a/communicate4.html] (accessed 5 July 2012).

Teens and the internet – screenagers

Belcher, K. 'Bullycide' – a sadly new pandemic. *The Mirror*, 3 November 2010. Available at [http://fairfieldmirror.com/2010/11/03/%E2%80%9Cbullycide%E2%80%9D-a-sadly-new-pandemic/] (accessed 18 April 2012).

Crabbe, M. Reality and risk: Pornography, young people and sexuality. Available at [http://www.parliament.vic.gov.au/images/stories/committees/lawrefrom/isexting/subs/S30_-_Maree_Crabbe_-_Attachment_1.pdf] (accessed 13 June 2012).

Eckholm, E. Six teens charged after classmate's suicide. *New York Times*, 30 March 2010. Available at [http://www.nytimes.com/2010/03/30/us/30bully.html?pagewanted=all&_r=0] (accessed 12 August 2012).

Educating boys about pornography. 2012. Available at [http://www.raisingboys.com.au/articles/post.php?s=2012-02-27-educating-boys-about-pornography] (accessed 14 July 2012).

Englander, E. 2006. *Understanding violence*. Lawrence Erlbaum Associates Publishers.

Freedman, M. 2012. Sex ed gone wrong. Available at [http://www.couriermail.

com.au/ipad/mia-freedman-sex-ed-gone-wrong/story-fn6ck8la-1226419798493]
(accessed 2 August 2012).

Gregston, M. 2007. *When your teen is struggling*. Harvest House Publishers.

Gregston, M. 2009. *Parenting teens in a confusing culture*. Believer's Press.

Grolnick, W.S. 2003. *The psychology of parental control: How well-meant parenting backfires*. Taylor & Francis e-Library.

Grolnick, W.S. & Pomerantz, E.M. 2009. Issues and challenges in studying parental control: Toward a new conceptualization. *Child Development Perspectives*. Wiley Online Library.

Grolnick, W.S. & Ryan, R.M. 1989. Parent styles associated with children's self-regulation and competence in school. *Journal of Educational Psychology*.

High, B. 2007. *Bullycide in America – Mums speak out about the bullying/suicide connection*. JBS Publishing, Inc.

Moore, D. 2010. Managing social bullying and aggression among adolescents. Available at [http://nmschoolhealth.org/documents/2010DOHRelationalAggressionHandout.pdf] (accessed 10 July 2012).

Pomerantz, E.M. & Grolnick, W.S. 2005. The role of parents in how children approach achievement. In A.J. Elliot & C.S. Dweck (eds), *Handbook of competence and motivation*. New York: Guilford Press.

Providing bullying and cyberbullying research, programs, and resources. Available at [http://webhost.bridgew.edu/marc/] (accessed 17 July 2012).

INDEX